Resilient

A Key to Being Brilliant!

Compiled by

Dr. Amanda H. Goodson

&

Daniel Scott, Jr., PMP

Resilient: A Key to Being Brilliant!
Compiled by Dr. Amanda H. Goodson and Daniel Scott, Jr., PMP

Featured authors (in alphabetical order)
Ashley Dickerson-Hall
Sonya Drayer
Dr. Amanda H. Goodson
Marlon Harmon
Rukiya Higgins
Ucheonye Maple
Dr. Stephanie May
Daniel Scott, Jr., PMP
Odetta Scott
Clifton Wesley
Veonicca Wesley

Editing: LLVE, LLC, Dr. Yvette Rice
Cover Design by Jan Hammond
Typesetting by Inktobook.com

Published by Amanda Goodson Global, LLC
Printed in the United States of America

ISBN = 978-1-951501-19-8
Ebook ISBN = 978-1-951501-20-4

Acknowledgments

Dr. Amanda Goodson

I'd like to thank my family for their continued support in my endeavors to write, speak, train and coach. Along with so many other things that I have the opportunity to be blessed to do. My husband Lonnie, you are such an amazing man, and you are perfect for me. To my son Jelonni, thank you for loving me how I am and allowing me to love you back. To my mom, sister and extended family thank you so very much for being there for me always. Je're thank you for your tireless support to everything I do!

Daniel Scott, Jr., PMP

I am honored to be part of a wonderful group of co-authors and was blessed to have been asked to support this amazing project. Special thanks to my family, friends, and mentors who continue to inspire me to live my purpose!

Ashley Dickerson-Hall

To my husband Corey, thank you for being my biggest supporter. There is no other person I'd rather be on this journey with. To my toddler boys, Caleb and Atticus, thank you for your endless energy, as you both keep me going. You bring me so much joy, and I am honored to be your mommy.

To my Gran, my Mama, and my Tete, thank you all for your prayers and unconditional love.

To my mentors, Beth and Tammy, your wisdom and counsel have been a vital part of my life. Thank you for pouring into me.

Thank you, Lord, for blessing me with my tribe and giving me the opportunity to share like-minded ideas with such awesome co-authors.

Clifton Wesley

I will state that writing is not my expertise but has been a rewarding experience. This opportunity would not have been possible without my wife Veonicca' Wesley, who introduced me to this experience. I'm eternally grateful to my sister Keonna Greene, cousin Robin Owens, co-worker Shahidah Harris, and Dr. Yvette Rice for your great proofreading skills. Thanks to my life-long friend "Joe" for allowing me to share your story.

To my parents, Curtis Wesley, Mary Terrell-Allen, Dr. Barbara Odom Wesley, and Olish Allen, thank you for the patience and hard work it took to raise me. Lastly, to my daughter, Elizabeth Wesley, thank you for being you, and my motivation to succeed be *Brilliant.*

Dr. Stephanie May

I cannot express enough thanks to Dr. Amanda Goodson and her team for their support and insight in completing this project.

Much love and many thanks to my husband, Robert C. May, and my sons William and Stephen May, for allowing me time away from you to research and write.

And finally, I acknowledge my parents, the Late Deacon Billy Joe Jackson Sr., and Mother Nellie C. Jackson; you are my inspiration for all that I continue to accomplish in life.

To all my friends and family, I say thank you.

Veonicca Wesley

Special thanks to my motivational team that has planted positive seeds throughout my life. This book is dedicated to these individuals. They are my loving and encouraging husband and daughter, Clifton and Elizabeth Wesley. The other four members of the "Fab Five" my parents, Rodney and Frenetta Greene, and my two sisters, Virnetta Woodbury and Keonna Greene. Without your support and the many mentors, coaches, family members, friends, church family, and extended family that have sowed into my life, I would not have developed into the person I am today.

Rukiya Higgins

Writing this chapter was harder than I expected; however, it was more rewarding than I could have ever envisioned. I would like to first thank Dr. Amanda Goodson for inviting me to be part of this project and affording me the opportunity to step out of my comfort zone to share my personal story of resilience; I am eternally grateful. To my grandmother, who walked with such style and grace, thank you for giving me the confidence to strive and aspire big.

Additionally, I would like to thank my mother and brother for their unwavering support and encouragement during the writing process. Thanks for giving me the space to take on this challenge. Lastly, this would not have been possible without the support of my best friend, who was entrenched in the process with me from start to finish and everything in between. She read every draft, provided critiques, and reminded me of the most important nuances to my story; I thank you!

Sonya Drayer

I want to thank my family for all the love and continued support for all of my adventures and endeavors, no matter how wild or big they are. Thank you to my closest and dearest friends who challenge me to grow and go beyond my fears to be the greatest version of me. Finally, thank you to all of the souls who have come in and out of my life. Each of you have taught me through experience and guided me through life's lessons and journeys. Each of you continue to allow me to be myself and encourage me to go after my dreams.

Acknowledgments

Ucheonye Maples

Special thanks to my husband- Jomo, my kids–Xavier and Jalen for believing in my when I had doubts; my mom–Linda, whose faith is unwavering and my beloved sister–Sherri, who taught me how to believe in myself.

Marlon Harmon

This opportunity would not be possible without the help of my pastor Dr. Amanda Goodson and her invitation to join such an incredible team of accomplished authors. Thank you to my wife Lisa, daughter Je´re, and son M. Quincy Harmon who always put up with me working endless hours on this project and other work that I am a part of.

My greatest inspiration comes from the Deltas of Mississippi, where my maternal family is rooted. This book project for me regards the generational resiliency that runs in my bloodline. This is a toast to our future.

Thanks all.

Odetta Scott

First and foremost, I thank God for this opportunity and all others that He has afforded me. I dedicate this book to my village – Daniel, my spouse, my family, friends, mentors, sponsors, and coaches. Thank you so much for pouring into me and helping me push and extend beyond where I could even see. Lord, through this work and all I do, I give you the glory, honor, and praise.

Table of Contents

Foreword

WHEN I WAS approached to participate alongside the amazing authors whose stories of resilience are captured within this book, I was flabbergasted. Each author is accomplished, brilliant and resilient in ways I have not experienced. Then, I had the pleasure of meeting them. I felt that I was already part of the book, amongst my tribe of resilient optimists!

As you read each chapter, you will see a common thread. You will discover that you have learned many of their lessons, you simply haven't realized it until you saw it written on these pages.

I encourage you to reflect on your own life as you read and absorb each lesson. How can you apply what they have learned into your life? How can the lessons be directly applicable to your journey? Have you learned similar lessons that you initially disregarded? I am a strong believer that God prepares us for all challenges in our lives.

In 2014, I was in an auto accident that caused a Traumatic Brain Injury. For 25 months I was trapped within my mind unable to speak more than a few simple words or walk without assistance. The hiatus I was forced to take allowed me immense amounts of time to examine the choices I've made throughout my life.

My "Ah-ha" moment came as a vision of my seven year old self jumping a concrete storm ditch. I promised myself, the universe and especially God that if I was permitted to speak and walk without assistance, I would live with the courage of a seven year old. I would dare to push through my insecurities, live a life of joy despite my fears and to share my lessons with others so they too would stop apologizing for what they aren't.

Within months of gaining my ability to speak and walk again, I was diagnosed with breast cancer. This time, I didn't lose myself. I had already been stretched further than I thought I was capable. Yet here I was, facing another battle. I reflected on all the stories I remembered while trapped in my head. I had mapped thousands of scenarios to the question, "What would I do if...." One of those scenarios was, "What would I do if I was diagnosed with cancer?" When the doctors asked me what my choices were for each step through my cancer process, I was ready.

The power behind resiliency is to understand that there is a way. You much choose to get up, keep moving forward and find your way. My mentor, Dr. Paul Scheele of Scheele Learning, once told me that if children approached challenges with the mindset of an adult, we would be a world of crawlers. Children are naturally resilient. When learning to walk, an infant will pull up, fall. Pull up. Fall. They keep trying until they perfect the ability to stand, then they begin practicing the first step. Imagine the world where we all kept getting up when a challenge was presented to us and even after the bruises, we still took the first step. Embrace your toddler mindset. Be the naturally resilient person God built you to be.

The knowledge I garnered through my trials has propelled me to complete the healing of my spirit. Another key to resilience is to have compassion for yourself. We fall and fail. We make mistakes. We are human. Demeaning yourself for errors that you never plan to repeat is a punishment you do not deserve. Allow yourself grace. You may have changed, but you are a better version of yourself from enduring the experience.

"My mission in life is not nearly to survive, but to thrive; and do so with some passion, some compassion, some humor, and some style."

–Maya Angelo

Part of my thriving through life is to guide others to rediscover their inner child that believes in miracles, dreams and most of all... themselves. Stop apologizing for what you aren't and be the best version of yourself every day. Be Unapologetically you!

Michelle Mras

International Speaker, Communication Coach, Trainer, Published Author, Podcast Host & Internet TV Host of Mental Shift on TNC Now

Introduction

OBSERVING HOW DIFFERENT people rise above and beyond their circumstances can open our understanding to how resilience produces brilliance in our lives. A quote that resonates rising above and beyond our circumstances is "There is brilliance in boldness." In most cases, resilience requires boldness to get beyond the circumstances and challenges we face. Thus, being resilient is a key to being brilliant.

We chose to write this book to assist people in exercising resilience and in helping them bounce back from adversities and challenges. The co-authors of this book have found ways to exude brilliance and manifest success beyond the challenges they have experienced. By writing this book, we hope to create velocity and momentum for others to learn tools to manifest victory in the face of struggle and hardship. We are all products of resiliency and the convergence that we all go through. Regardless of our backgrounds, economic or socio-academic statuses, age, race, or gender, we must have the courage to conquer adversities and challenges and move beyond them. Overcoming adversity is a journey, and the ability to prevail over adversity is a process. What we choose to learn from our trials underwrite future successes. As we share our individual strategies, we hope that our brilliance created from resilience opens your understanding of your inner brilliance.

There is a common theme throughout this book. How will we show up after the trial or adversity? Will we show up wounded and hurt? Will we show up angry or hostile? There is a connection between who you become and how you show up after adversities or challenges. Resilience causes us to show up well regardless of what happened to us, what we experienced, or what happened around us. There is a cliche that says, "I don't look like what I have been through." What do we look like after the storm?

Additionally, there is reciprocity when speaking of resilience and brilliance. Resilience produces brilliance, and brilliance produces resilience. Studying the elements of a person being resilient, we see their inner brilliance. When others demonstrate their brilliance, their stories usually include episodes of resilience when faced with tough times. The ability to develop the forethought, fortitude, and character to withstand trials produces the brilliance that shines for others to be enlightened. These brilliant people become a beacon of hope or a north star for others. Their energy can pull others up from their challenging circumstances to a place of hope and expectancy.

Brilliance does not come without its challenges. While resiliency or its brilliance is challenging enough, some people are not as accepting of this brilliance as others.

A word from Daniel

I discovered everyone who is with you is not always for you. I pride myself on being an authentic leader and believe that authentic leaders exhibit great character and trustworthiness in the face of upheaval. As an authentic leader, I have set the bar for brilliance much higher than the bar that is set for me by others. Even when others thought I was not good enough, I exceeded their expectations through determination, perseverance, and the brilliance of resiliency. Resilience is a core tenet of my life and helps to define who I am. Because of it, I show up triumphantly for every challenge and integrate the lessons I learn into every future endeavor. I pass those lessons on to others so they can have the forethought to conquer failure and adversity that happens in their lives.

We know that people have learning differences, not disabilities; they learn from different perspectives and spectrums. We also recognize that society is normalized in a particular way. When a person exceeds a scale or bar erected by others, it becomes an issue or stumbling block for those who erected that bar.

In our society, we have intellectual geniuses, physical geniuses, or mathematical and musical geniuses. Unfortunately, we have a group of people who are not being reached, and their brilliance has been hidden because of the normalizing bar society has tried to leverage. Like Dr. Amanda Goodson, these people have been told they were not smart enough, yet their brilliance and achievements far exceeded what others said they could achieve. Hint: her story lies within the pages of this book.

As you read further, it is our desire to pull that brilliance out of you that others have tried to normalize and suppress, offering the fullness of who you are by exploring your true selves. Don't believe the lies others have spoken over you, especially those words that were used to dim your brilliance. You are not what others have negatively declared.

The nine other co-authors of *Resilient: A Key to Being Brilliant* chose the path of vulnerability when sharing their stories of failures and successes because they recognize the importance of authenticity. There is relatability and adaptability in each of the stories shared because these authors are aware that they are all "yet becoming," meaning there is still a work in progress in each of their lives.

Authors Marlon Harmon, Ucheonye Maples, and Rukiya Higgins overcame dysfunctionality in their homes, families, or workplaces. Authors Odetta Scott and Veonicca Wesley share how an illness/injury redirected their focus to achieve brilliance and build others up along the way. Sonya Drayer and Ashley Dickerson-Hall encourage mothers with their courageous stories of parenting. From a single-parent perspective to one that includes the responsibilities of marriage, both women faced challenges in the marketplace relative to motherhood. Dr. Stephanie May and Clifton Wesley's stories regarding the importance of generational legacies of resilience in the African American Family cause readers to research their family ties to learn about their ancestors' stories of brilliance.

Every chapter of *Resilient: A Key to Being Brilliant* will motivate you to choose boldness over timidity, resilience over complacency, and hope over discouragement. Although we may fail in certain instances, we are not failures. We have been created to take those times of missing the mark and use them to elevate us to higher levels of success because resilience and brilliance became intertwined. We are all in the middle of becoming someone brilliant, so do not allow your emotions to tell you that you have not done well.

Read on to discover your inner brilliance produced through the resilient times in your life. Learn how to show up victoriously after your storm through established processes shared by the authors. Get ready to proclaim to the world, "I don't look like what I have been through, but I do have a successful story to tell."

Yes, Resilient is a Key to Being Brilliant!

Dr. Amanda Goodson
Daniel Scott, Jr., PMP

1

Brilliance Defined and Realized

Dr. Amanda H. Goodson

WHEN I LOOK at brilliance, I look at the facets of peoples' lives that make them strong and unique. An excerpt from a book expresses my thoughts best: "A person who has a personal persona, a brain that identifies them as larger than life." Brilliance is the thing that makes you shine, the thing that makes you strong, and the qualities that make you unique. It could be behavior, or it could be how you engage in the room. Someone once told me that when I walk into the room, I walk in tall. It's not only about my height – but it is also about the presence that I bring. So, when I think about brilliance, I think about what you bring to the room, the patent you have on society, and how you bring your greatest strengths to do something well, where you shine and where other people notice when you shine.

Brilliance was not immediate; it was a process that took time. I grew up thinking that I couldn't. I was told so many times, "You can't do this. A woman can't do this, and you can't do that." Then I discovered what my name meant. The name Amanda means *worthy of love*. Once I understood that I was worthy of something, and that was the name that had been given to me at birth, the level of brilliance started to show.

There was also an *aha* moment which began via a process of things. I started seeing that I brought things to the table that no one else did. In my mind, this began to form the strategy to do something nobody else had ever done, to do it in a way they had never done it before, and to do it where I would be needed and noticed. As I started sitting in that seat, I began to recognize that brilliance was there. Instead of me competing with someone and trying to be like them, I tried to be the best me that I could be. That was done by bringing things to the table that nobody else could bring. The feedback that was received was that they had never thought about what I had presented. This was also a part of my strategy—to get to a place, sit in a seat, present something in a way that had not been thought of, and then bring my best self.

I grew up watching certain television shows and cartoons. When I became a professional, my television shows became C-Span and the like because I wanted to learn about the people leading the world – how they dressed, how they talked, and the types of conversations they were having. There were times I got an opportunity to be in the room with Congress and listen to congressional hearings and to some of the people who were leading our country and leading NASA. I saw how they operated, and I started to emulate them. In doing that, I could plant what was learned in places that were right for me. When I took a look around and realized the line I was in was short, it seemed right for me; I became passionate about it and decided to stick to it.

The Role Resilience Plays in Discovering Your Best Strengths

The role of brilliance gives a practical application of how we can be different. As we start discovering what we're good at and what we're strong at, we then become teachers of excellence. At this point, we are becoming resilient, and we can help other people become resilient. As our organized thoughts become aligned with our best strengths, we will have reached the layer of being an overcomer. This is where resilience is realized.

You now start noticing your passion and discovering the things that are applications of your strategy and how you are teaching them. This shows resilience. Because you have become a teacher, you have overcome. And at that place of being a teacher, you can now see the slice where you become the master of situations – not the master over people. Embedded in that scenario is how you play resilience. It's similar to a musical note. If you're playing music or if you have ever played a musical instrument, or if while singing in a choir and you see people play an instrument, there is a note that resilience plays and it has a particular key. As you discover your best strengths, there is a note, or a score, or a melody that resilience plays in helping you to get where you are to be and to where you are transformed to be.

The Individuals Who Inspired the Discovery of Brilliance

It started with people in the community. I had a teacher named Mr. Rogers who lived right down the street and would drive us back and forth to school in his van. I loved math growing up and used to play little math games. Whenever my parents would be driving to different places and I was bored, I would make mathematical equations, factorials, or multiplication problems from the license plates. Later in high school, I entered a math competition and finished in the top ten at #8 [the number for new beginnings]. The principal announced the school's new winners of the math competition over the loudspeaker, and then he called my name. I was in class at the time, and everyone commented on how he had called my name. It was weird for me, but I remember on the drive home, Mr. Rogers said, "Congratulations. I heard your name over the loudspeaker and that you got 8th in the math competition. That's a big thing." That was what I needed to salt and pepper my direction.

Then there was my father. He was the reason I became an electrical engineer. He would tell me, "Baby, with the way you like to live, you need a career where you can make a lot of money because you don't need anybody to take care of you when you get older." So, I did some research, and engineering sounded pretty good. In the beginning, I thought I wanted to become a musician since I played a little piano; however, I realized that wasn't my best suit.

Other great individuals were those such as my mentor Dr. Laura Thompson and also Dr. Myles Monroe. With Myles Monroe, I wanted to hear from him personally. I got on a plane and flew to Florida to attend a conference near Ft. Lauderdale, since he was known all over the world. It turned out we were in the same hotel, staying on the same floor, and I was near enough to his voice. I bought every book I could get and all the media he had. I knew he had to come through the lobby's main door, so I sat in the lobby until I saw him come through that door. I got up and decided to tell him that I only came to Florida from Tucson, Arizona, for him. He was with his wife at the time, but she stood back so we could talk. I told him I read all his books and heard him speak in Tucson. I told him that after hearing him speak on the Kingdom of God, I couldn't sleep for about 3 days because I had never heard anything like that before. His response was, "That would be about right. You keep going in that direction because that's important. God will work with you. That's what happens to people when they learn, and that's important." So, I often tell people to try and meet the people who will affect their lives and go and get the resources – even if you have to scrape and scrap. The resources are there to help you in following your passion.

Another individual who was my mentor while working at NASA was named Wiley Bunn. I would go into his office, and he would give me assignments. Each time I thought I had done my best work, he would find a flaw or something wrong with it that needed fixing. Since he was older and wiser, it never occurred to me that he would always find something wrong. But that was his way of seeing how I would respond. Every time I went into his office to talk to him, my goal was to always have the answer to any question he might ask. That required thinking about and discerning what he would ask on every particular subject under the sun. I also ensured that my products were stellar so I would be ready for him. He once said to me, "You did a lot of work in this, and you prepared for me, didn't you?" Then we had an opportunity to talk, and he asked me about my goals, aspirations, and about the job I wanted. I responded that I wanted his job, but not that I wanted him to lose his job; only that I wanted him to move up. He was at the Senior Executive Service level and in charge of Quality in Mission Assurance. He said that I would have to work harder than everybody else, that people would not like me and be envious of me, that I would have to travel to places I never thought I would have to travel. He also said I would need to work during the times of day and night that others would not be working, and I would have to be willing to relocate. He then asked if I would be willing to do all of those things. When I responded yes, he told me that he had been looking for someone he could mentor and that he was glad that I was willing to do all of those things. Over time, I did get that job.

Many others have also helped me discover my brilliance – Dr. Yvette Rice, my team, and my parents. I have purposely tried to take nuggets from all of those influencers to help me become the person that I believe I am becoming. Through that process of becoming, I am apt to pivot – to go up, go around, go down, and go in, although sometimes it is hard. What I've learned is that sometimes I can't always just go through the front door. If there is an opportunity, I may have to go through a window. If I see a crack and my foot can get in there, then the rest of me can get in there. My thought is – all I need is a crack. I don't always have to walk in a door with everything I have, with all of my power and might. I have seen people being promoted and displayed on billboards and everything, knowing that I am being promoted too. God then says to me, "I didn't reserve that for you. What I reserved you for is for you to transcend with anybody and anything that you could ever think or imagine. And I'm going to do it in a way that is suited for you."

The Most Resilient Person and Their Key Strategies to Becoming Great

The most resilient person that comes to my mind is my son, Jelonni Goodson. He has a unique way of thinking, and of how he processes information and data. When he was five years old. I called for emergency assistance and then rushed him to the hospital where he had to go through all types of tests. The hospital staff kept asking how I was doing and wanting to get started doing all their tests; my son said, "Mom, let us pray."

He has had many challenges, where people have said he couldn't do a certain thing and where he didn't measure up to their standards. He spoke to me once, and I asked him how he deals with that. He said, "I get to a point where I don't see how good they are and compare it to me. But I see how good I can become compared to myself. Once I make the measure of the people, then I've missed the opportunity to be better because, at that point, I start feeling bad about me. But once I see that I can be better in a certain way, I don't measure myself against them; because that does not help me to be the best me that I can be."

Jelonni now has two degrees – an associate degree and a bachelor's degree, all achieved while taking extra time to take tests, extra time to do work, and with people telling him that he couldn't. That did not stop him. He never stopped, nor did he say that he felt bad and didn't want to do it. Not even with students making fun of him and his work and telling him that his work wasn't as good as theirs. He never let that any of that stop him from getting his degrees, his diploma, and doing the work that he needed to do.

This is an example of the most resilient person that I have ever met, and I've known him all his life and seen him go through all that. Jelonni thinks differently; he processes differently, and his brain is known to be different. I never told him that he was less than anybody else. I told him that he processes differently and thinks differently from others; then, he found a way to leverage that.

The Keys to Influencing the Discovery of Individual Brilliance

The key to influencing the discovery of your individual brilliance is to PUNT:

P Promote yourself to think outside of the box and think from the standpoint of seeing yourself outside yourself and walking in a level of brilliance.

U Understand that you are uniquely made, and you are uniquely you. You bring something to the table that will make an indelible impression on eternity that no one else can bring. Start writing about those unique things—the things that people told you that you weren't good at and those things you were told you couldn't do or shouldn't do a certain way. After writing it, start to see how the rosebud begins to blossom and open up, and shows the brilliance in you.

N Never give up; never give out, and never give in. Never giving up means you understand that you are unique. Your uniqueness will birth brilliance. When you never give up, then that means you keep trying. To never give in means not giving in to the hype, the hurt, or the complexity or perplexity of it. In not giving up, you will reach a level of understanding that other people will not pursue. An example of this is seen in watching a race in the Olympics. Some runners will stick their nose out and will win by a nose. The question is, what does that nose represent for you? What is that little bit that you give that others cannot and have not given? That is where you start discovering your brilliance.

T   Think differently about your outcome. You are here, and you were made to be a solution to a problem. You are a solution to an organization. You are the solution to a process. You are the solution to a system. You are a solution to your community. Know where you must bring a solution to a problem. Start by noticing the problem; then start noticing your passion; finally, start seeing the solution.

This is what speaks to the key to your individual brilliance.

The Plan for Becoming More Resilient During the Time of Crisis and Strengthening Those Skills

When we look at the world crisis, we typically think of negative things. I have learned that some cultures have a different definition of the word crisis. When looking at the closest definition, it means opportunity. Dr. Cindy Trimm teaches that opportunity has a language. As we start to understand that crisis means something different for different cultures, we take ourselves out of the cultural norm that has held us back and held us down, which catapults us to a place of opportunity. That's how I plan to be more resilient – to speak the language of opportunity, take the chances, and then measure the opportunity versus the risk of what I should not do. I look at the glass as being half full rather than the glass being half empty.

You must plan. You cannot just walk into it. Planning means that you think about it beforehand, and it means that you've got a strategy and a thought. So, now my thoughts have to be connected differently today from the thoughts that I had yesterday. And even if I may not change one thought or a set of thoughts or standards today from what I did yesterday, that helps me become more resilient and leverage that opportunity.

In that, I must practice because, as some might believe, practice makes perfect. However, someone once said that practice makes permanent. So, I practice this new behavior, I think about it, and I say here is where I need to put this piece of the puzzle. When putting a puzzle together, you will have a piece with a 90-degree angle; that is a corner. Pieces having the ridges and the swirls are not part of the corner; they are not the foundation pieces; they are the pieces that go on the inside. The key is getting those foundational pieces. That's what people do – they work on the foundation before starting to work in the middle. Becoming resilient during a crisis is the same thing. I find out the boundaries and the edges and those things that frame my masterpiece, which helps to leverage the opportunity. Then I make plans to put these pieces of the puzzle together.

An example is the work I have been doing with a coach who has me strengthening my muscles. She has me stretching first and doing certain things. I cannot just pick up the heaviest weight on the first day of training. She is working me up to it. I started out doing things on my knees before even doing real push-ups. I still can't do the push-ups, but she is taking me little by little. When I started working out with her, I had the expectation that if I was not feeling well, continuing to work out would make me feel better. She said, "You can't cheat working out. You have to bring 100% of yourself – even when you're working out to get the best from it." People often cheat the work-out when they come to the work out. So, when we're strengthening our skills, we think we're supposed to pick up the heaviest weights first. NO – you must start with the lighter weights before you can get to the heavier ones. Also, know that your arms are not as strong as your legs. I found out that I'm out of breath more when I am working my legs because those are bigger muscles. When you are doing big things, you are working big muscles, which will take more strength.

When you come to the table and are not bringing 100% of yourself, you don't strengthen your skills to become a more extraordinary leader. What you are doing is strengthening yourself to become a mediocre leader because you are bringing a mediocre effort. When you give no effort to it, expecting something to be given, then you get no growth. And if you put a little effort into it, then you get a little growth.

To strengthen yourself to become the best you can be requires that you bring 100%; you can't bring 70%, and you can't bring 80%. I used to tell people that if you're too tired, then just bring 80%. But when you bring 80%, you only receive 80%. However, if you bring 100%, you will receive 100%. That means you must work out 100%, but you also have to rest 100%. You've got to bring your best self to the game – the best that you are that day to wherever you are. That's how you strengthen your skills to become a great leader.

Once when I had to do a presentation and didn't know the subject well, I looked at videos online, videos at work, and videos that other businesses had. I literally looked at every word they said and typed it up to engage with my brain. I took a piece from each, put it together, made it my own, and then I recorded it. I would listen to myself no less than 20 times – all for a 5- to 7-minute presentation. I looked at the best of the best, wrote myself out a script, and then practiced doing it. I then listened to my recorded script. I listened to it while in the shower, putting on my clothes, walking up and down the hallway and the steps – all this while others were sitting around eating Oreos and watching other things.

When it was time for the presentation, I was on point. My boss, who is the Vice President, sent a note to me and said I made her proud, just like a proud momma. Others said that I crushed it and knocked it out of the park. One even said that it seemed as if I had been doing this job for 20 years. In actuality, I had only been there for four months. They had no clue that I was burning the midnight oil. I did rest, however, knowing the importance of getting rest. I was up at 3 or 4 in the morning practicing – because practice makes permanent.

Every time you come, it's a dress rehearsal for excellence, and with resilience, you can bounce back from anything. Just change the thing you are doing in the outcome, and then decide based on the consequences—not on the glam that you see. Know there is a consequence based on the decision that you make. Start making decisions based on the long-term effects, as well as the feel-good type of thing. I advise people to consider what matters ten years from now or twenty years from now and then ask them to choose today what will matter twenty years from now.

This is how resilient people think. Brilliant leaders think brilliance, and resilient people think with that type of strategy. Be consequence-driven; be opportunity-focused; then take the chance based on a future outcome and a tactical execution today.

Discovering Your Purpose by Navigating the Ridges to be Successful

When looking at my passion and my strength, people began telling me that I was really good at this. I started looking at my calendar and the types of people that started getting onto my calendar and then looking at the kind of problems I had resolved. That navigated me to my purpose.

The ridges are navigated by understanding that I don't have to be perfect every day. This is the practice piece. I discovered my purpose by examining who was getting onto my calendar. I then started to discover my purpose by the people I really admired, the passion that I had, and then how I was able to apply things well.

I up-scaled myself to plug into that purpose. The discovery was similar to putting together a presentation for a science project. 'Amanda Goodson is this type of person.' 'Amanda Goodson is that type of person.'

The Greatest Challenge and Turning that Challenge to My Advantage

My greatest challenge was how I thought. It was my thinking. I practiced daily telling myself how I couldn't do something. I was in a type of tug-of-war. It is your heart that teaches you what you believe and what you value. This is innate to everyone when we are very young. Your brain establishes the goal and then envisions the thing. My greatest challenge was the competition that I was creating within my values, beliefs, and thinking. I began to understand that they all need to complement each other. There is a cross-section where your values, your brain, and your beliefs cross and intersect. That's how I learned how to soar.

My greatest challenge was how I thought about myself and how I sought the vision of how I saw others. I had a myopic view of leadership; I had a myopic view of what I was doing and becoming, and I had a suppressed vision of myself and my capabilities. I never saw that, if I stepped right outside of that box by a nose or by a hair, that everything would then change. So, the most significant challenge was getting the complement of my heart to my head. Once I got that complement, and my heart and head were engaged at the point where they intersected, there was no stopping me.

The Role Played in Helping Others to Become More Resilient

People often call me wanting to meet for only a few minutes. Some will take ten or fifteen minutes, and others will take an hour. One young lady called me, stating she had talked herself out of getting onto my calendar, but then one day, she told herself to take a chance. Taking a chance is also a language we should learn, but many people don't discover that language. When someone takes a chance and gets on my calendar, they have a mindset of what they see. I will ask for their permission to speak to them from a different perspective to help them see something different. Then I get them to agree and catapult them to another place.

The role I play is to ask them to agree to be different and get into cadence and in alignment with a new way of thinking. Once I have that agreement, I then give them a different view – to turn it around and see another piece of the tapestry or another piece of the puzzle and that masterpiece. This is because they are not focusing on that one small piece when it's actually the whole ocean available to them that's out of order. I get them to think differently, and I get them to shift their thinking and augment their current reality. This is what catapults them to a future benefit.

Key Takeaways in the Shift from Plan to Purpose

The key takeaways make me think about SHIFT:

S See yourself as better than you are. See yourself as a becomer, not as an arriver. That means that you are still becoming, and you are still transforming.

H Have a success-oriented mindset. Have thoughts of success, creativity, innovation, and emotional wholeness. Have that mindset before you show up in the room. Your mind should already be there. I have long feet, and I used to tell people that my feet would enter a room before the rest of me.

I Innovate- – early and often. Innovation is key to who you are purposed to be.

F Find you. We are often busy finding other people and who they are, and we can even read them up and down and write a book about them. Find you and do you.

T Tenaciously pursue it – when you find you. This is the point where you discover that you won't have any competition; it becomes irrelevant, and you create a capability that will plug into a source that will lighten up the room.

The connection you make with your heart and your head – those two points – makes a difference and creates tension and compression. Once you start to bring those two points together, that tension lessens, and you don't have competition with yourself. Then, once that tension lessens, you will see yourself starting to move up and out and into a different space.

Dr. Amanda H. Goodson is a groundbreaking aerospace engineer who soared to become the first woman to hold the position of Director of Safety and Mission Assurance out of the Marshall Space Flight Center at NASA. Transformed from a young African American girl who was told by her teacher that she would not amount to much, Dr. Goodson uses her unstoppable "can do" spirit to inspire others to achieve their goals regardless of the obstacles.

Noted nationally for her achievements, Dr. Goodson has served on the Board of Director's Chair for Advancing Minorities Interest in Engineering (AMIE), in addition to serving in leadership positions for a Fortune 500 aerospace company. Dr. Goodson is also the senior pastor at Trinity Temple CME Church in Tucson, Arizona.

Contact Information:
amandagoodsonglobal@gmail.com
website: amandagoodson.com

2

Adversity & Failure are the Resilient's Playground

Daniel Scott

I AM VERY appreciative of the opportunity to discourse on resiliency as it is a part of my very essence. Being my authentic self, I intend to inform, provide humor, and provoke thought. I am evolving. Being resilient is all about progress...

I am that guy. I have it all: a beautiful wife, wonderful children, a great family, and a lovely home. I have worked for 30 years in commercial, aerospace, military, and defense. I have led people and processes. I have managed businesses upward of $200M. I am a leader and have held various titles: director, technical director, business development director, and general manager. I am a mentor, coach, advocate, and ally. I have various certificates, college degrees and am in pursuit of another.

While I am incredibly successful, I have also experienced failure...

...I am also that guy who grew up in a place with one of the highest murder rates in America. I am the one who got kicked out of catholic school as a kid...the one who broke my leg and had a body cast on for three months. I failed out of a top-ten engineering school in America; yes, I got 4 F's in one semester. I have not had money to feed my family or myself. I have had challenging relations with my family. I have been divorced. I have been audited by and owed money to the IRS, laid off, not once but twice. I am an enigma, a multitude of strange, puzzling, incomprehensible, yet wonderous facades. Any of these feel familiar?

In addition to experiencing failure, one of the characteristics that describe me most is that I am resilient. Resilience, in this instance, is the process of successfully adapting when faced with adversity. I describe it as the process and ability to transcend from a state of challenge or, in some cases, the ultimate challenge: getting through adversity and failure.

"Without struggle, there is no progress."

– Frederick Douglas

Similar to Frederick Douglas' quote, I believe "without stress, pressure, or failure, there is no growth." These experiences, at some point in everyone's life, are resolute. Stress, pressure, and failure are facts of nature. Consequently, resilience is not only the ability to bounce back from failure but also, more importantly, to learn and grow. As resilient leaders, we should strive to succeed and fail, learn, and develop.

Trust the Process

There is a wealth of academic pedagogy on resilience – articles, books, journals, and many TEDx Talks. A significant number of these artifacts discuss some sort of process for which a person becomes resilient. My approach is listed below.

Let's face it, adversity and failure are but a small part of life. They are but two of life's dynamic experiences. Contextually, hardship, loss, and failure have always been looked down upon. If I did not win, there was no trophy for second place. When I grew up, albeit in sports or school, I was programmed to compete and win. When I went off to college and got 4 F's in one semester, I got kicked out of college. When I joined the Navy, I was rewarded with the best job if I got the best grade in my electronics class. If I did poorly, I got what job was left. If I failed, I was sent to the fleet with limited options for employment. Even in the participation trophy generation, the second, third, or fifteenth place trophy is valueless without acknowledging the challenge and the lesson or process of overcoming the loss.

As human beings, we face many challenges. Set-backs are a part of life. Failure can be painful. No one sets out to undertake a challenge to fail. However, as leaders, we must recognize that these challenges provide the basis for motivation, passion, and inspiration. Success does not mean you are successful at all times in all things. I have never known one leader who has been genuinely successful at everything, at least not one leader who will confidently look me in the eye and tell me so.

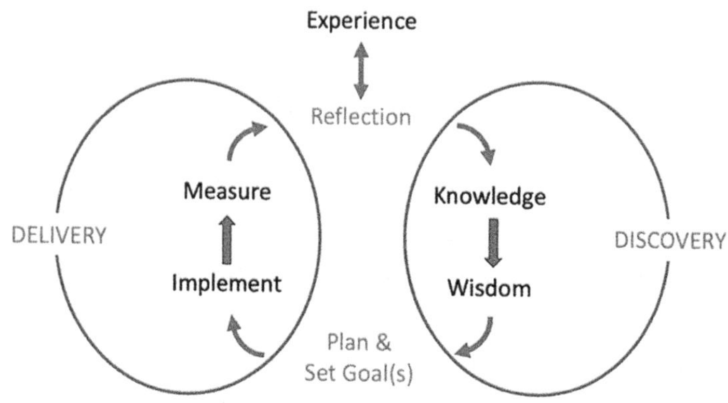

Figure 1: Resiliency Leadership Characteristics Method
Copyright © 2021 by Daniel L. Scott, Jr.

Resiliency, or at least my method model for it, shown in Figure 1, comprises four steps: reflection, discovery, planning, and delivery. When I experience adversity or a state of challenge, I take time to do some intentional review. This reflection is sometimes by choice and other times by force. Nonetheless, critical thought is a mainstay in my life. The first stage of a good leader is to realize that failure is a part of life. Stuff happens...and all the time. Renowned philosopher, John Dewey, theorized the tenants, concepts, and benefits of reflection over 100 years ago. Leagues of philosophers and scholars have dissected and deconstructed his work since he published his works on reflection.

As this is a leadership book and not a literature review, I will summarize that reflection should be intentional, create purpose, root itself in inquiry, and be communal. Resilient leaders are seekers of understanding, archeologists of knowledge. By archeologist, I mean we should intentionally look at the present failure and the history of how it occurred and analyze its artifacts (reasons).

Next, in reflection, is to create purpose. Simply stated, resilient leaders strive to understand "the true why" and give meaning and purpose to the suffering of loss or failure by taking and applying lessons to the next project, next endeavor, and next experience. The reflection of the adversity/loss/failure provides learning to be used in the future such that the failure can no longer be repeated. Too often, as resilient leaders, maybe because of the sting and the newness of the situation, we examine the direct cause of the failure without fully and profoundly recognizing the root cause. Understanding "the true why" is the step of the inquiry. Understanding what happened, how it happened, how I contributed to it, how the environment contributed to it, or how opportunities were missed to pre-process or in-process fix what was ultimately going to happen is all part of reflection. As a resilient leader, I have done these several ways, i.e., solicited advice from my manager, team, peers, customers, and leaders. Sometimes I got advice even when I didn't ask for it nor want it. I also sought to get inputs from outside of my sphere of influence – mentors, coaches, and suppliers. This communal feedback is crucial to a resilient leader–no matter how painful. Remember, feedback is a gift.

The next step in the method is discovery, which includes knowledge and wisdom – turning this newfound reflection into understanding and applying it into practice. What could I have done differently? What if this challenge presents itself again? How might I apply my review and learning to new situations? Where does this new knowledge fit, and where does it not? Leaders who have inspired me have had significant challenges. They learned from the challenges and adapted to become better leaders. These leaders have inspired me and others by being transparent in their short-comings and show how they have grown as leaders by turning failure into success.

< Commercial Break >

Resiliency is not just a space for the adaptation of reflection, discovery, planning, and delivery. It is also a platform for utilizing courageous resolve when stressed, turning disap-pointment into triumph, or controverting a sense-of-loss into a sense-of-contentment or sense-of-fulfillment—for example, my son, N'aithan. A very thoughtful and highly intelligent young man, as well as a good athlete, N'aithan persevered in pursuing his dreams of going to college, representing the United States in the Olympics, and learn-ing how to fly. He graduated from college, having gone to school on a track scholarship. After graduation, N'aithan trained and was a successful Olympic hopeful, securing major endorsements. Just before the Olympic trials, he was injured and unable to recover. Once fully recovered, N'aithan joined the military, where he took private flying lessons. All of his dedication paid off as he not only got his private pilot's license, he was able to continue to inspire his family by being selected to become a military pilot. The lesson I learned from N'aithan is that "*I CAN* is 1000 times more important than my *IQ.*" This example is but one vital lesson I have learned from my children. They were all raised to be leaders – resilient leaders, and the lessons that each has taught and continues to teach me are invaluable.

< Now to return to our scheduled program >

"Everyone has a plan until they get punched in the mouth."

– Mike Tyson

The next step in the method goes hand-in-hand with wisdom; one should put together a solid plan and tangible goals. It's not that you face a stressful situation or face distress: hardship, fear, anxiety, remorse, sorrow, guilt, apprehension, dread, or trepidation; how you respond to it defines you. Resilient leaders understand that happenstance is not a plan. To face adversity, create a plan of action. In my darkest days, when I have gone through hardship, failure, or loss, through pain and anguish, no matter how big or small, I have, in some cases, painstakingly created a plan. This plan is a plan of action. It lists activities, owners, dates (when possible), and goals. A list of actions without owners and dates is just a list of actions, similar to a grocery list. We are hungry, but who is going to store and when. If my goal is to make lasagna tonight, I need to ensure that someone goes to the store before dinner to get pasta, sauce, eggs, and cheese and not peanut butter and jelly. Without the perspective of who needs to take action, when the actions need to be taken, and the setting of the goal, the efforts fall short. If there is no pasta available, then "plan B" would be peanut butter and jelly. Why, because as I already said, "Stuff happens."

The next step in the Resilient Leadership Characteristics method is delivery, which is composed of implementing the plan and measuring progress. I am reminded, fondly, of two sayings that relate to delivery – from the Bible, James 2:26, "Faith without works is dead," and, author unknown, "that which gets measured, gets done." How does one go about implementing a plan – very intentionally and consciously. Implementing a plan should be very deliberate. When I got laid off – the second time, the experience was somewhat daunting. I had a great title and reasonable financial compensation. The job just was not a good fit for the company and me at that time. I had a great team, and collectively, we performed better in the face of significant opposition than I had anticipated. Either by nature or nurture, I am a planner.

Initially, when I took the job, on every interview, I stated to everyone who would listen, "I plan to go back to school to get my doctorate." Wanting to live my purpose-driven-life, I have known for 20+ years, my purpose is tied to education. Ultimately, my purpose is to inspire and influence others to "be" and live their purpose; but I digress. I knew what school and what program, but I was on the grind for five years working for this company. I had three positions and moved three different times in that period, yet, my burning desire to get closer to my purpose still burned. So, with the onset of the global pandemic amidst the environment of social change, I implemented my plan for going back to school. Hence, I wrote out steps for when I would apply, who would write my letters of recommendation, which I would talk to in administration, and students who were either in the program or recently graduated. Each step would need to be accomplished. I executed the plan, monitored each step, and communicated the plan with my stakeholders (my internal board of directors). Ultimately, I was accepted to each of the schools for which I applied. As a project manager and general manager, so much of my career has been a measure of delivery skills. It was only natural for me to program manage my applications to graduate school.

My Resilient approach can't be completed without starting where you began or finish where you start – reflection. Once you have delivered on the plan derived from delivery and initial reflection, one should think critically about the change and the growth that comes with it. Initially, I talked about how reflection should be *intentional*, create *purpose*, root itself in *inquiry*, and be *communal*. Did the process yield intentional change, growth, and development? Did the discovery yield a plan of action when implemented, and was it measured for growth and development? What are the lessons learned about yourself that will be taken into the next experience? Despite the adversity or failure, trust the process and, even more importantly, trust yourself!

Daniel Scott is a son, brother, uncle, husband, father, coach, mentor, and leader who exists to inspire and influence others to serve their purpose. He is a jack-of-all-trades with 30 years of professional experience including leadership and management in engineering, operations, contracts, general management, business development, and Six Sigma process improvement. Daniel is also a proud submariner who served and qualified on U.S. Navy submarines, and he was an officer in the Civil Engineer Corps.

Contact Information:
dlscottjr1914@yahoo.com

3

The Resiliency of Navigating Motherhood and a Career

Ashley Dickerson-Hall

Beyond its traditional meaning, I characterize brilliance as a creative and skillful way of thinking that presents solutions to problems. Relative to my life experiences, brilliance also represents something or someone who illuminates light. That shining light may be presented as a different approach to navigating various situations, whether professionally or personally.

I was born and partially raised in Chicago, Illinois. Brilliance and resiliency were intertwined in my life, even as a child. Due to my childhood circumstances, I was forced to discover the importance of resiliency early. Growing up in the inner city required a different strength that most children do not find until later in life.

For instance, Chicago has the nation's second-largest public transportation system. Many of my 2nd and 3rd-grade friends rode public transportation to school instead of riding school buses. These friends were exposed to incidents that required the ability to protect themselves. Because of their experiences, I realized I needed to learn how to protect myself and survive if I faced similar encounters. I also recognized that I needed to know how to recover or bounce back if something similar happened to me.

I believe we discover brilliance through resiliency when we encounter the need to overcome a circumstance. That's when we uncover our greatest strengths. While living in Chicago, my siblings and I grew up in a low-income neighborhood where crime scenes were the norm. For young children, we witnessed so much beyond our years. The ability to navigate beyond the environment of that inner-city life took brilliance I didn't realize I had. At the age of 4, I moved to Decatur from Chicago. My sisters and I would go back to Chicago to visit family during summer breaks. At the age of 7, my sisters and I moved back to Chicago for what we thought would be permanent. Although we started a new school and gained new friends, it was still a transition. In Decatur, we attended public schools, but we attended a Catholic school once we moved back to Chicago. Since we lived in the inner city, my mother was very particular and sought out the best education for my sisters and me. My teacher was a nun, and I wore uniforms to school every day. This was completely different from any school experience I had in Alabama. However, I was able to adjust, and I was an honor roll student. They say children need stability and a routine to thrive. But, they also say children are some of the most resilient people and can adjust fast. As a young child navigating through different school systems in various cities, I can attest to this.

Eventually, my siblings and I were relocated to a small town in Alabama. Decatur provided a new environment where I felt sheltered and protected. At that point, I sensed I could let my guard down and be a little girl again. Fortunately for me, we moved in with my maternal grandmother, Peggy Grisby. My "Gran," as I fondly call her, played a critical role in me discovering my inner brilliance. She saw some things in me at an early age that I couldn't see in myself. Never doubting my capabilities, my grandmother constantly assured me that I would make it and I would grow up to be somebody great one day.

Gran was adamant about the company I kept and the path I took in life. She knew that associating with the wrong people would send me down a destructive trail that could negatively affect the brilliance within me. Gran played an active role in my life, and I was not allowed to engage with my friends in activities that I thought were "cool." She was firm and did not want me to make some of the same mistakes she made when she was younger. Gran made it her duty to surround me with brilliant individuals full of wisdom.

Oddly, at the age of four, my best friend was an elderly 80-year-old woman named Mama Mandy who lived across the street from us. Mama Mandy and I visited daily. She became a second grandmother to me, even allowing me to have slumber parties at her home. Mama Mandy was very wise, and she used the game of BINGO to teach me basic arithmetic. I also learned the fundamentals of finance and having a savings account through Mama Mandy. The game's rules were simple: I couldn't play BINGO if I didn't save enough pennies. Mama Mandy did not believe in IOUs or gambling with "a broke four-year-old." She was lively and well able to keep up with me even at her age.

Pre-Kindergarten was a breeze for me. If I was not light-years ahead of my fellow kindergarten classmates, I was definitely 80 years ahead of them! Unlike the streets of Chicago, between Mama Mandy's house and my Gran's, I always felt the warmth of a home life.

Even though I lived a sheltered life with my grandmother, she also taught me the importance of being independent and not expecting a handout from anyone. Under Gran's guidance, I learned the value of hard work and integrity. Her value system was crucial to me understanding the importance of resilience, leading to many successes as an adult. However, there are times when those strong independent characteristics hinder me from reaching out to others professionally when I need their brilliance to help me navigate through a problem.

The Resiliency of Motherhood

When I think of all the resilient people I encountered throughout my life, the ones that influenced me the most are mothers, whether they bore the children or volunteered to rear them for other reasons. Childbearing and childrearing change every aspect of a woman's life, including her dimensions of wellness, physical body, emotions, intellect, and finances. These components are altered over a short period of nine months when bearing a child. Yet, women are expected to bounce back and recover their physical and mental state immediately after the newborn arrives.

There are so many physical changes that come along with a pregnancy. The most obvious is weight gain, and weight, unfortunately, is not always distributed evenly across the body. Although I experience substantial hair growth while pregnant, I suffered tremendous hair loss after giving birth to our son. I was enormously self-conscious due to the weight I gained and the hair loss. I struggled with thoughts of not being able to recover because of the stretch marks and body aches.

Additionally, I went through spiritual changes. My prayer life shifted, focusing on being restored to the woman I was before giving birth or accepting those life-altering side effects if I did not recover. I also prayed that I would be able to cope with my new life.

When starting a family, work-life balance is essential. Depending on the vocation, some women make career sacrifices that affect their family's finances. At the time of this publication, I have been a consultant in the medical device industry for 10 years. My career allowed me to see the world.

Pioneering as a Working At-Home Mom

In 2017, I had an opportunity to work on what I considered a "golden project" with one of the largest pharmaceutical companies in the world. I would travel for two years between Ireland and Belgium while spending a few months in the United States. This project was client-based during a time when remote work was not highly excepted or popular. Shortly after the offer, I learned I was pregnant. I ended up declining an opportunity of a lifetime in my career field to ensure a safe pregnancy. It was a bittersweet moment for me, but I knew I made the right decision for my health and my child.

I struggled emotionally about my decision to walk away from that opportunity, creating an immense amount of self-doubt. I was unsure how that choice would be perceived in the consulting industry or how my decision would ultimately affect my career. I was afraid that I would lose the high visibility I worked so hard to gain as a consultant. I questioned whether I was that resilient woman.

At that time, I had not heard of many consultants who were mothers in my industry because of the massive amounts of travel required. Some of the women I worked with were married, but they did not have children. I enjoyed my career, and I was passionate about it. But I was not sure how I could balance being a new mom and a consultant. Even though I wrestled with my decision, I believe my key strategy to being resilient was remembering the "WHY."

Motherhood is my most significant challenge to date. However, I now realize those challenges made me a better person and more resilient. I feel honored to be a mother, and I am thankful the Lord blessed me with children. The choices I made worked to my advantage. After combining motherhood and a career, I consider myself a "world-class" multitasker.

Reflecting on the time from stepping away from my career after childbirth to three years later, the restoration of things in my life was far more than I could imagine. Resiliency evolved into added strength for parenting and a career.

Parenting involves steep slopes, sharp turns, and the ability to navigate while being studied closely by your observant children. As a parent, I am mindful that how I steer and recover through life's experiences sets an example for them. There are times when I look back at some of the situations I faced as a parent and laugh because of the strength I gained.

Once I realized I was ready to return to consulting, I became creative in sharing the role of motherhood and being a career professional. In 2017 I gave birth to my first son, and in 2019 my second son joined us. I worked remotely for 2 years, and when my youngest was 5 months in September of 2019, I began traveling for work again. My Gran agreed to meet me in Boston, Massachusetts to help with the transition. Since my youngest son was only 5 months, I decided to bring him along for the journey. My oldest stayed home with my husband and continued to attend childcare. My grandmother kept my son during the day while I worked, and I would come back to the hotel to nurse and give her short a break. We did this for a month until the project changed to remote status. It was tough! But we made it, and I don't think I could have made it without Gran. I sought opportunities where I could work from home years before the COVID-19 pandemic. I asked the consulting firms about the clients' perspectives and would they be willing to allow me to work offsite. I expressed how this scenario could save the clients some money by eliminating my travel per diems. Brilliance and resilience joined forces on my behalf because some of the companies agreed to my request. In those instances, I work from home most of the time after attending the client's required training.

Mentorship, Coaching, and Brilliance

It is critical to be surrounded by brilliant people who want to see us thrive in discovering our individual brilliance. The thoughts of my grandmother reminding me of the importance of the right inner circles influenced my decision to seek others who could assist me in discovering the brilliance within. I met the challenge of my new lifestyle with the help of accountability partners and mentors.

I was introduced to my lifetime mentors, Yolanda Beth Harris and Dr. Amanda Goodson, through my best friend, Ma Mandy. Ma Mandy was Beth and Amanda's grandmother, and I now consider them part of my family. A little girl from Chicago, I am now surrounded and embraced by more brilliance than I could ever imagine. When we are encircled and nurtured by brilliant individuals who hold us accountable, refusing to let us settle, it is easier for us to discover our brilliance. It literally took a village of intelligent women to guide me in the path of discovering my virtuosity.

Another key to discovering the brilliance within is deciding to never give up. Learning to bounce back may not happen the first time we are faced with a struggle. However, at some point, there will be a breakthrough that overcomes the situation. The critical mandate is being persistent and getting up when we fall. In hindsight, the Covid-19 pandemic was my breakthrough. It guaranteed me remote work so I could be home and care for my babies. I was ready to give up on consulting and go back to Corporate America, as it seemed to be a better fit for the "traditional" 9-5 working family. But coincidently, and just when I was ready to give up, the world "stopped." Travel was banned, and I was forced to work from home. Some days, I felt God stopped the world just for me to parent and provide for my family simultaneously.

During these unprecedented times of the COVID-19 pandemic, the world is faced with navigating through a new normal. There was not ample time for us to plan the intricate details of the requirements to survive and thrive through this crisis as a society. However, during the pandemic, we discovered dormant strengths and talents inside us that we used to become teachers for our children, home-chiefs, entrepreneurs, and authors. We learned that some skills and abilities are discovered through force.

Taking advantage of virtual classes during a crisis like the pandemic is another excellent opportunity to gain knowledge, sharpen our skills, and make additional self-discoveries regarding our strengths. The technological advances developed during this time provide new ways to network and socialize, opening the door for fresh possibilities.

I see myself as a life-long learner. After becoming a parent, I realized gaining wisdom from experts relative to my personal and professional life was critical to traversing beyond my current circumstances. As an independent consultant, it is my responsibility to find my next contract. The components of being a wife, mother, and career professional all contribute to the contracts I choose.

There are times I miss traveling to beautiful places throughout the world. There are also times I crave adult interaction while working from home. But I remind myself that the choices I make while our children are younger are temporary. They will mature into young adults who do not rely on their parents as much. Until then, I depend on reputable professional networking platforms that educate, connect, and challenge me.

During the pandemic, I also discovered that my years of experience working remotely provided a platform to help other women adjust to their new routines of juggling work and educating their children simultaneously. I became their mentor related to the resilience of navigating motherhood and a career during a pandemic. I was their role model, helping them to discover their brilliance while remaining resilient during circumstances beyond their control. I taught them the value of living one day at a time and remembering this situation was temporary. However, we must still perform at our maximum potential to complete the job.

I believe God graces us for every challenge as working mothers. Even when many in the marketplace do not extend the needed grace to women who choose a career and motherhood. Sadly, some women do not find their work-life balance because of this stigma, so they forfeit their promising careers. This phenomenon has been more prevalent during the pandemic.

With our first child, I hid my pregnancy for as long as possible because of the awkwardness I felt and my career advancement concerns. I finally talked to my client when I was seven months pregnant. I knew they hired me to fulfill a task, and I wanted to complete the work. Fortunately for me, I was allowed to start my first remote work opportunity for the final months of my pregnancy.

An Example of Resilience and Brilliance

I have five younger sisters. I always felt it was my responsibility to set an example for them. Gran did an excellent job of stretching her money to take care of us. We grew up in a small 3-bedroom, 2-bathroom home where we shared beds. Although most of our clothing was secondhand or might have been handed down from the older sister, we were clean and neat girls and always had a hot meal to eat. We were on government assistance, so we all understood "the value of a dollar" at a young age. Yet, my siblings and I never felt like we were without.

I always knew there was more to life. Growing up, I had a desire to see the world and learn about other cultures.

When those doors open for me to travel internationally, I took the time to share my experiences with my siblings because I wanted them to be inspired.

One of those occasions to travel came through a youth trip to Canada. This trip was the catalyst for my desire to travel and explore the world. I yearned to see more of God's beautiful creation. It does not matter what circumstances we are born into; we can excel beyond them. We are placed on this earth by God with a purpose.

That same young girl born in "Chi-Town" and grew up in an overcrowded, 3-bedroom home on the northwest side of Decatur was chosen to be an exchange student and travel to Japan my senior year in high school. This opportunity came through a partnership with Daikin America Inc. In preparation, I took Japanese etiquette classes to prepare for the three-week experience.

The only African American in the group was a culture shock for some of the young Japanese children who wanted to touch my skin. I indulged in exotic Japanese cuisines and sushi wrapped to perfection. Imagine that same young girl whose meals were once provided through US government food stamps was resiliently traveling the world and efficiently eating with chopsticks.

I believe God used this occasion to prepare me for the future career opportunities I received. The resilience I developed as that little girl in Chicago and the lessons learned from my Gran ignited an attitude within me that I could do anything. After high school, I attended the University of Arizona, graduated with a degree in Engineering Management, and minored in Biomedical Engineering. Even though I passed on that first golden career opportunity, I now work for some of the world's top Pharmaceutical and Medical Device companies.

RESILIENT: A KEY TO BEING BRILLIANT!

Resilience is a mindset and a choice. We must decide daily that we will get up and do whatever is necessary to overcome any obstacles in the most creative and efficient way possible. Sometimes it will take longer than we anticipated. But we must be persistent and consistent with reaching that goal, remembering that those obstacles are temporary.

We must think of ourselves as a rubber band. After we are pulled and stretched, we eventually realize we still are not broken. Thus, the only thing left to do is to snap back into shape and perform. That is resilience!

Ashley Dickerson-Hall is a native of Decatur, AL and currently resides in Dallas, TX. With over 10 years of experience as a Quality Engineering Consultant, Ashley has provided regulatory and compliance consultation to some of the most advanced Medical Device and Pharmaceutical companies in the world. When time allows, Ashley enjoys traveling with her husband and exploring God's beautiful creations with their two toddler boys.

Contact Information:
Adickersonhall@gmail.com

4

Life's Resilient Toolbox

Clifton Wesley

IT IS IMPORTANT that any handyman/woman completing a task knows what is in their toolbox before starting work. However, as additional tasks are given, or problems are encountered, they might need additional tools. This idea is symbolic of the two terms resilient and brilliance; terms, often associated with life's success. It is important to note that not all the tools present in the box are positive. Some are negative and the result of challenges and obstacles experienced throughout life. Through the analysis of the items in the toolbox, one's life can be dissected. To better understand the toolbox, we must understand what brilliant means.

According to Webster's New Collegiate Dictionary, the word brilliant means "distinguished by unusual mental keenness or alertness."[1] In this context, most individuals think of brilliant people or those who stand out. However,

---

[1] A Merriam-Webster®. *Webster's New Collegiate Dictionary.* (2nd ed.). G. & C. Merriam Co. 1974.

my technical background allowed me to construct a definition; it is someone with technological capabilities, mental toughness, and the ability to bounce back from missteps and mistakes. It is impossible to define brilliance without using attributes associated with resilience. It is safe to say that resilience is a process that comes through growth and evolution. Just as with any project, a handyman/woman must recognize that it is human nature to be fearful, but it is possible to remove your fears if you have a strong sense of faith which will allow your motivation to increase.

Remove Your Fears

The idea of self-doubt and believing that one is not adequate leads many to be fearful. Therefore, it is vital to REMOVE YOUR FEARS. I have experienced this firsthand through the observation and guidance of mentorship. One of my mentees, an engineer, decided to take a leave of absence to go back to college and obtain an MBA after working ten years in her profession. She felt that the engineering vocation was no longer viable for her. However, after earning her MBA, the mentee decided to return to the company. I needed help on a program, so I reached out to her because I knew she had the desired capabilities. At that point, I encouraged her to believe she could be a successful engineer. As a leader, I use the "reach one, pull one" approach of providing opportunities and coaching to help others find their brilliance.

During the program work, I discovered that fear hindered the mentee from utilizing her full competencies. Fear was her obstacle to experiencing a brilliant engineering career. Moving beyond the apprehensions, this mentee is now a system's lead on the program, assisting her direct reports into discovering their brilliance. Engineering skills can be taught. However, the confidence to recognize one's capabilities and brilliance must come from within. The idea of removing fear has allowed brilliance to exist. It requires the ability to fill in the white space and the unknown. Brilliant innovators are not intimidated by the unknown.

For me, being resilient is the ability to adjust and recover. I understand that no one is perfect; mistakes will happen, whether by commission or omission. How I react to those mistakes is based on my ability to cope. In the case of the mentee in my organization, it was fear of not recovering from a mistake that was holding her back.

From lessons such as these, there are instruments placed in life's toolbox that prevent making the same mistakes again. We must learn not to hover around the missteps but learn from them. This lesson was instilled in me at a young age as my mother constantly told me that my success came by recognizing and observing my older siblings' mistakes. When I saw their blunders, I knew I did not want to go down the same path.

In addition to learning from our own and others' mistakes, we must assess the knowledge from history's faults. My young daughter expressed her distaste for history. I shared the importance of learning from the past because it reveals where we have shortcomings and success. Studying history reminds us not to repeat the mistakes of the past, while it presents the opportunity to build on the success and failures of the past.

To truly overcome one's fears, it is essential to admit that shortcomings are not a sign of failure. Instead, it presents growth opportunities. It is important to note that no one excels in everything. Therefore, it is vital to use the many resources provided to aid us in reaching our potential. For example, in my own life, I enjoy certain activities. Still, to become as successful and productive as possible, I utilize YouTube videos relating to woodwork, lawn care, and golfing. I gain practical knowledge that leads to personal improvements in those areas. Every learning opportunity produces resilience.

Find Your Motivation

In life, there are many ways to FIND YOUR MOTIVATION. For me, this motivation is demonstrated through my past, present, and future. This message of motivation transpires throughout generations and is the direct result of lessons learned and obstacles overcome. In order to provide you a better understanding of motivation in relation to brilliance, three different areas of people will be utilized, my family, friends, and professors. In addition, I will explain how a summer job changed the entire course of my life. I was finally very motivated.

The first category is finding your motivators and cheerleaders. Although you might not agree with everything they do or say, they look out for your best interest. They are the people you can count on in good and bad situations. For me, this came from family, my mother, Mary Terrell-Allen, and my dad, Curtis Wesley, and my bonus mom, Dr. Barbara Odom-Wesley, my dad's wife. They make sure to never let me down, and I always wanted to make them proud. They were there for me through all the sporting events and academically through the good and bad grades. Their consistent effort to raise me into the person I've become gave me the fortitude to never disappoint them.

The patriarch side of my family has been very influential in molding and motivating me. As a result, I have found motivation from my father and my Uncle Herbert, both goal setters. The legacy was passed on regarding hard work and sacrifice by them and my grandfather, Clemon Herbert Wesley, Sr., a sharecropper. My grandfather advanced from being a tenant farmer who received living arrangements and food to work someone else's land to owning land and a small farm.

My grandfather raised hogs and used the proceeds to pay for his children's education. They all attended Prairie View A&M University, a historically black land-grant university in Prairie View, Texas. My father majored in Mathematics, and my uncle in Electrical Engineering. Both my dad and Uncle Herbert took the knowledge and legacy my grandfather passed to them and expanded the vision. My job is to take what I have been given and enhance it for the next generation. These men influenced me to pursue brilliance.

The next generation and one of my greatest motivations and joys in life is my daughter Elizabeth. As a father, I have seen her transition from a shy, quiet little girl to now, an outgoing preteen. Throughout her life, she has always been small in stature. However, I have always encouraged her to reach for her dreams and never let her size hinder her from accomplishing her goals. Elizabeth demonstrated this lesson learned as she entered middle school. She decided to try out for the middle school basketball team and play one of the largest instruments in the band, the baritone. She made the basketball team and is one of the top baritone players. Just witnessing Elizabeth's success, I am reminded of the seeds I plant daily in her life, as well as others. As a result, I constantly strive to set good examples as a father and demonstrate to her what it takes to be brilliant in this world.

Secondly, motivation comes through life challenges. I saw this first hand from one of my dearest friends who attended Prairie View with me. I consider him as one of the most resilient people I know. To respect his privacy, I will call him Joe. Joe's birth mother passed away when he was about eight years old. His mother's oldest sister raised him, whose life included hustling as an occupation, leading to her living an abusive lifestyle.

It was typical for Joe's home to be raided because of drug sales. After the last raid, his aunt vowed to quit selling drugs, so she took him on a shopping spree because of her expected lower income. This shopping spree occurred when Joe was in the 7th grade. His aunt purchased clothes and shoes that were too big for him to accommodate his potential growth. Joe brought those same clothes and shoes with him to college along with a $20 Sprint calling card.

Removing himself from poverty was Joe's biggest motivator. While growing up, Joe chose to go to schools out of his neighborhood because he felt he would have a better opportunity to escape poverty if he were in an integrated middle-class school environment. Even in college, Joe made sure to build relationships with people whose mindsets were above his and who would keep him motivated. Joe never looked back; he always focused on his future opportunities. He is now a level three partner at a major consulting firm. That is resilience and brilliance demonstrated.

The final category is people who are motivated based on opportunities provided to them. Three of my college professors, Dr. Freddie Frazier, Commander Taylor Kelly, and Dr. Kendell Kirby, provided my opportunity. They came to my rescue when I lost my scholarship due to immaturity. These individuals found greatness in me when I had difficulties accepting them myself. They told me I was too smart to be making the poor grades I received. These professors encouraged me to treat college like it was my job. My classes from 8:00 am to 6:00 pm became my work hours. The time I was not in class during the day was set aside as study hours. This schedule allowed opportunities to meet with my professors during the day if I had questions I could not solve. Foolishly, before their intervention, I relied on other students in the class to teach me things they didn't understand themselves. After my professors' mediation, my grades were never lower than a 3.2 GPA (grade point average).

Dr. Frazier also provided me the opportunity to tutor Calculus. I was able to earn money, take responsibility for my success academically, and learn the criticality of mentorship. I also worked in the engineering lab at the college, where I conducted environmental testing. My professors obliged me to attend the Black Engineer of the Year Award (BEYA) Conferences and participate in their job fairs. A recruiter from the former Hughes Aircraft Company interviewed me. When he saw my lab experience from Prairie View, he offered me an internship which led to full-time employment and my present career. It was the vision of my professors who saw brilliance in me that afforded me this opportunity.

The idea of a wasted opportunity was shown as I lost my

scholarship at Prairie View. I remember calling my dad and asking him to put money on my account to register for the next semester of school. My father remained calm because he expected this situation to happen. I left home with a car and new freedom, headed to a college with beautiful young women. My dad put the money in my account. He didn't show signs of anger, but I could hear the disappointment in his voice. However, I believe my dad knew that at some point, something would inspire me to navigate and find the brilliance within. This brilliance would be found that summer. My dad, and my bonus mother's dad, Elzie Odom, got together and found me an internship. The internship involved a group of college students working for a Portland Cement company. Our job was to keep the extremely fine powdered cement from hardening on the ground or the machine. Weighing in at 125 pounds at the time, I worked with a 75-pound jackhammer in my hand. Even with the outside heat, I was required to be completely covered with long sleeves and pants. Life was miserable.

An older gentleman on the work site told me one day, "I can tell you are an intelligent young man. You don't want to do hard labor for the rest of your life. You do not want to be 50 years old, making $40,000 a year. You can come out of college at 22 years old, put on a suit, and go make $40,000 a year working in an office." I believe my dad and my grandfa-ther, Elzie knew this job would motivate me to get me back on track to improve my grades and finish school. I realized what I didn't want to do, so my goal became, get back in school at Prairie View, make the grades, and go after the job I wanted. My thoughts were, "I loved math and science. Why not get paid for doing what I love?" After that challenging experience with the cement company, tools for success were added to my toolkit. I became highly motivated to finish school and earn a good-paying job.

Find Your Faith

As I navigated throughout life, I have added good and bad things to my toolbox that have aided me in discovering the brilliance within me. Throughout this time, I have relied on my faith. As a result, I consider myself a present-day warrior of resilience. I grew up during the times shortly after desegregation in the United States. While in elementary school, I was the only black student in my grade for two years. Going to college at Prairie View was a refreshing opportunity to see a room full of minority students excelling. As I reflect on my positive and negative experiences at Prairie View, I knew God had me there for a purpose. It was in His plan for me to be there. My constant reliance on my faith has allowed many opportunities to open for me. As a result, I move forward without fear, knowing that God will continue to provide growth opportunities for me.

This faith in God and confidence in myself have allowed me to make significant decisions during the COVID-19 pandemic. As a leader, I was responsible for ensuring calmness in our organization. I was able to rely on my faith as well as my people skills to make major decisions. I was able to adjust and not stress over the fear of change. I recognized that tension and anxiety were at an all-time high. Therefore, I believed that family should come first, and I knew fathers and mothers on our teams that schooled children from home due to the pandemic.

Additionally, our teams were spread out across the United States. While working from home, it was important for team members to take lunch breaks. I designated a specific time for lunch and encouraged employees to step away from working to take mental breathers, read, eat lunch, or spend time with their families. Also, there were no meetings scheduled during that timeframe. During one of the breaks, I ordered pizzas throughout the country for the team members and their entire families.

There were, however, crucial deadlines that needed to be met during the pandemic also. Some situations required working late hours, but I still tried to create a work/life balance. Empathy is a critical component of leadership, and brilliant leaders recognize the need. My faith is the piece in the toolbox that reminds me to be humble and compassionate.

Toolbox: There Is Always a Little More Room

In the toolbox call life, I have found that there is always room for a little more. This includes the good and the bad. With every lesson learned, a piece of you is placed in the toolbox. However, it is essential to close it for reflection and celebrations sometimes. There have been many challenges that we had to overcome just to progress in life. Nothing done should be neglected, no matter how big or small. We should never forget to draw on the legacies and people that have helped pave the way to us reaching our present state. At the conclusion of the day, tangible things such as money are not real motivators when a person already lives a comfortable lifestyle. Secondly, I find things that motivate me and use them to my advantage. From the things and people that inspired me to go to college to present motivators such as my wife, Veonicca, and daughter, I keep striving for the best.

Additionally, there is a difference between optimism and resilience. Optimism sometimes means a person has a dream, but the navigating tools to accomplish it are undefined. When resilience is part of the navigating process, the goal is quantifiable, and the navigated course to achieve the objective is well-defined. To define the motivation, I would ask myself, "If I don't do this, what are the consequences?"

These takeaways continue to be viable for unpacking our toolbox.

- Remove your fears
- Find your motivation
- Find your faith

Do not allow fear to hinder you from brilliance. Use that fear as a motivator to brilliance.

In addition to technical capabilities and resilience, brilliance requires reading between the lines to understand the problem and develop a solution. Whether it is a technical or personal family problem, the capability requirement is the same. This ability moves beyond following standard operating procedures and being instructed through each step of the process. Brilliance requires the ability to fill in the white space and the unknown. Brilliant innovators are not intimidated by the unknown. They are trailblazers looking for a better product, method, and idea to shift the future in the industry and in life.

Clifton Wesley is an engineer, innovator, business leader and family man. Clifton has distinguished himself as a leader of technical teams across a 24-year career in the aerospace industry. He is truly a force multiplier—demonstrating the skill and ability to maximize growth opportunities and contributions from the teams and projects under his leadership.

Clifton's is passionate about connecting his experiences with future leaders, wherever he encounters them. This passion has garnered accolades from the Tucson Boys and Girls Club as Volunteer of the Year, and the Black Engineering of the Year (BEYA) as a Modern-Day Technology Leader as he provided mentorship to their mentees to develop their technical and leadership capabilities.

Clifton has a bachelor's degree in Electrical Engineering from Prairie View A&M University and a master's degree in Systems Engineering from Johns Hopkins University. In his leisure time, he enjoys spending time with his family and supporting his beloved HBCU alma mater.

Contact: CWesley32@gmail.com

5

Educating Through the Challenges

Dr. Stephanie May

WHEN I FIRST heard the subject of this book, I immediately said, "if the topic is resilience, how does brilliance fit in?" Defining the word resilience has divergent answers relating to my life and career.

As an administrator and a mentor for thousands of students and teachers through the years, I have operationally defined resilience by how I act and react during troubling times. To be clear, we will always have disturbing situations, but we have the gift of experience. We are resilient when we power through those situations, realizing that we have made it through tough times in the past. Therefore, we have what it takes to make it through the current trauma.

Circumspectly, resilience takes on a different meaning when I think about what it meant to be raised in the deep south in the sixties. I watched my parents, the late Deacon

Billy Joe, Sr. and Mother Nellie Jackson, go through struggles just to make sure my siblings and I made it out of the horrific experiences they dealt with. I watched them work hard for minimal reward, compensation, or adulation. From that perspective, resilience means there was never a time when I heard my mother or father say, "I give up." However, the way they responded let me know, when life gets exceedingly difficult, there will be endemic challenges when you choose to exceed beyond other's expectations for your life. There will be some pushback.

Whenever there was a "fork in the road" in my life, my parents were there. There was just an abiding presence. Growing up, I never wanted anyone to say to me, "I am going to tell your Mom," because I made a bad decision or did the wrong thing. I always wanted to make them proud. Those are the kind of mentors my parents were.

I drew from my parents' experiences, and it propelled me forward. For me, that is the resilience portion. I now realize that after you go through the "refiner's fire" and all the rough edges are made smooth because of what you learned, brilliance is defined. I take the struggle and make meaning out of it by becoming an example for the students I can influence at various points in my life. Additionally, as an education administrator who supervised teachers, I realized that I could impact them as they watch me go through and respond to situations based on what I learned.

Applying those lessons learned is my definition of wisdom that only God can give. As an author in this book, I humbly accept the charge of the title of brilliance, but it comes with a cost paid mainly by people who came before me. Referring to my parents, they introduced me to brilliance at an early age. They were just one generation from slavery. My grandfather, Reverend James Samuel "Chuck" Carter, was the original pastor of Jones Chapel Methodist Church in Decatur, Alabama, in the early 1900s. When he passed away, the Methodist Conference gave my grandmother a $4 per month pension to live on. So, brilliance on making it through the difficult times didn't just start with my mom. My grandparents had to literary take nothing and make something.

Before his passing, my grandfather pastored two Sundays a month at Jones Chapel and two Sundays a month at Oakland United Methodist Church in Tanner, Alabama. Those two Sundays, my mother traveled with her parents to services at Oakland. According to Alabama Historians, the land for Oakland was deeded to its parishioners in 1879. In a "wooden one-room building," freed slaves worshipped and operated a private school to educate their children, producing ministers and educators. [1]

The Emancipation Proclamation did not guarantee education for freed slaves, especially in the south. Thus, the elders of Oakland wanted to make sure their children could read and write. Education was a means for their children to go beyond working in the surrounding cotton fields. My grandmother, Harriot Loveland Carter, became an educator because of the resiliency of the elders at Oakland and the elders in our community.

Recognizing that Loveland was smart enough to further her education beyond primary school, my great grandmother Ella Matthews, allowed her to server the plantation master's daughter which open the door for Loveland to go to

---

[1] Alabama Historical Association. A County Older Than the State-Limestone County. https://www.alabamahistory.net

high school and college. Loveland traveled to New London, Connecticut as a companion to the slave master's daughter. However, in her servanthood, she was able to attend secondary school, graduating as the only African American in her class. It was brilliance and resilience for my great grandmother to let her young daughter leave home. From there, Loveland attended Hampton University, receiving a degree in education.

For us, the church was traditionally the community's core, making it a place where we worshiped, learned more about God, and united when there was a need or concern in the community. Whether you were Methodist or Baptist, the church leaders of the community came together and used brilliance and resilience to overcome obstacles.

As a child growing up in Decatur, I remember the predominately black churches in the community providing makeshift daycare programs by offering Vacation Bible School over the summer. The same children traveled from Shiloh Missionary Baptist to St. James Presbyterian, to Jones Chapel Methodist, to First Missionary Baptist, and to Union Grove Primitive Baptist to receive free educational and biblical training in a structured environment during the summer months. We learned to read, report, and speak publicly about the biblical stories discussed. These skills development opportunities reinforced the importance of articulation and other orator competencies, preparing us for a future beyond what was offered to our parents.

Following in the footsteps of my grandmother and mother, I am a third-generation educator. As a chemistry teacher, I can relate to the scripture that says, "As iron sharpens iron, so one person sharpens another,"[2] because it takes personal experiences to help us ultimately find our best life. I came from a proud tradition of educating and preparing the next generation for what it will take to be successful. Like those who mentored me, I tell the up-and-coming generations to go beyond what they can see and dream beyond what doubters tell them they will never be able to accomplish. I was fortunate enough that my parents told me I could do anything.

The Resilient Educator

Many have credited my successes to coming from an intelligent family, or from having the most positive upbringing. However, others who came from the same family and had the same upbringing didn't necessarily process the experiences the way that I did. Some people that faced what I encountered growing up never went beyond the confines of a culture that included pressure to go and work in a factory. There is nothing wrong with blue-collar laborers. It is dignified employment. My father worked in a factory to take care of us. Yet, I felt at 18 years old that I would always be in Decatur, Alabama, if I did not leave Decatur. I sensed that the culture at that time would place limitations on my dreams. As soon as I graduated from high school, I left my hometown and went to college at Alabama A&M University in Huntsville. From there, I became a teacher and never returned to Decatur to live.

Being resilient helped me discover that I was more potent than the opinions others had of me. It enabled me to

---

[2]Proverbs 27:17. THE HOLY BIBLE, NEW INTERNATIONAL VERSION® Copyright© 1973, 1978, 1984, 20111, by Biblica, Inc.™. Used by permission of Zondervan.

remember who I was during the strenuous times as a teacher in the classroom. Some experiences were more difficult than others. After earning my doctoral degree, Stephenson High School in Georgia recruited me to teach underperforming science students. There were times in the public-school setting when children came to school abused, hungry, and angry. I had to push through those challenging moments to help those hurting students realize their own greatness. They were not just mad because they wanted to be angry. There were underlying issues that caused them to be angry, and it took time to get through to their actual need.

I then realized these students did not have the support of a community of churches that I had growing up. I may be the only Bible they read and the only church they see. So, I had to develop an inner peace that said, "if I just stay here and show them how much I care for them, I can give them more than what is in those books."

In addition to teaching them the content of the chemistry book, I made sure if the students were struggling readers, they would be able to read by the end of the school year. Whatever they needed to overcome, God made me an intercessor during those times.

I discovered the strength of patience as I relentlessly helped my students prepare for standardized tests. I was one of those teachers who could sit with the students one-on-one or one-on-ten to help them study for the end-of-course tests. There were testimonies from students that had taken the tests four and five times unsuccessfully that past after going through the after-school science tutorial program that I created. I saw resilience in each of those successful students, while others missed the opportunity to be perfected in an area of weakness because they gave up in the middle of their struggle.

Collaborating with my husband, Robert C. May (an Engineering Project Manager), we also initiated a competitive robotics program. In their first year of competing, the team won a trophy at the World VEX Robotics championships. Since the inaugural program startup, robotics was provided for all K-12 DeKalb County school children. These robotics competitions resulted in student scholarships and employment in computer science, robotics, engineering, and mathematics.

I am told that the significant moment in your life is the moment that you discover your purpose. I have been married for over 40 years, marshaled through the rigors of obtaining multiple degrees, including my PH.D., and reached a margin of success financially and professionally. Yet, even after retirement, my purpose continues as a teacher and mentor, and so does the need for resilience. Presently, I am anticipating another doctorate, as a life-long learner.

Resilience has taught me to be patient with myself. Even during the COVID 19 pandemic, I learned to enjoy the quiet time and to be grateful for life. In my estimation, my greatest strengths are yet to be discovered because I am still a work in progress. I understand that I am improving through continual growth and adaptation as I face new challenges.

INSPIRING RESILIENCE FROM ONE GENERATION TO THE NEXT

I know that I can understand and accomplish anything that I set my heart and mind toward because of the many teachers and mentors that embellished my life. However, my mother was the person that inspired me and helped me discover the brilliance within. She was my first and best teacher. I have a passion and a talent for music, education, and serving because of her.

My love for music was demonstrated by the creation of the Columbia High School Gospel Choir while teaching for DeKalb County, Georgia. The Inspirational Voices Choir's inaugural performance was for Black History Month. However, the choir's success led to a tour of Historically Black Colleges and Universities (HBCUs) throughout the United States and a performance abroad.

My mother was always in pursuit of more excellent knowledge and understanding. She greatly loved her family. I watched her become more devoted to us and her service work in the church and community after her mother, father, and my dad passed away. That was the epitome of resilience and brilliance. My mother blazed an excellent trail for my siblings and me.

Two other women who encouraged and mentored me were from my hometown of Decatur. Mrs. Clara Jean (Key) Johnson and Mrs. Ida Pearl Stone also reinforced my gift of singing and musical capabilities. From an educational standpoint, my high school chemistry teacher, Mr. Robert Henry, was very influential in my career path.

To date, I still believe my father is the most resilient person I have ever known. He was born an orphan because his mother died during childbirth. Today, some agencies provide financial and governmental assistance for children in need. However, this was not the reality for children of color born during the post-depression and pre-civil rights era of the Jim Crow deep south. For my father and his siblings, their grandmother and other extended family members did their best to keep them in school, out of jail, and in the church. By the time I was born, my father had graduated from high school, attended college, served in the military, and learned a trade. He was a master chef, a skill he was best known for.

One of my father's key strategies was that he never made excuses. He always had a desirable work ethic. He never missed a day of work, and for most of his life, he worked two or three concurrent jobs to take care of us. My father believed we would have to work "either our heads or our hands." That is why he made sure he placed something in our hands related to talents and gifts, including musical instruments.

My father's influence even passed down to my oldest sister, Quida. During the summer months, she created an improvised school for us younger siblings while my mother worked during the day. We focused on mathematics and reading. If Quida took French in school, she taught us French at home.

My father's strategic key guided me to develop keys of my own relative to discovering one's individual brilliance.

- Discover your worth by surrounding yourself with those who are stronger, smarter, and set high standards for themselves and for their inner circle.
- Develop a set of gratitude habits; saying thank you for what you have, writing in a journal the things that God has done for you, and telling others what you appreciate about them.
- Become a lifelong learner. Don't be afraid to try new things or to seek better ways to doing old things.

- Be willing to adapt when change is required.
- If there is something you want to do, stop making excuses for not getting it done.

Resilience and Brilliance in Times of Crises

Becoming more resilient was vital during the COVID-19 pandemic. From March 2020 to February 2021, we were blessed with the gift of time. For some married couples, this time presented a challenge. That eleven-month period was the first time my husband of over 40 years and I spent that much time together during the daytime. We learned to love each other all over again. Also, we developed a daily schedule to ensure that we continue to grow emotionally and spiritually.

The need for resilience and brilliance went beyond my household during the pandemic. The Bridge at Austin Community Center is our senior ministry for Bethesda Cathedral of the Apostolic Faith Ministry. Many of our seniors, before the pandemic, were regularly active, coming to our center daily for health and wellness classes, lunch seminars, and other learning activities. Prior to the COVID-19 pandemic, I felt highly effective as a face-to-face, one-on-one instructor. However, during COVID-19, the ministry had to pivot. On Sunday, March 15th, 2020, we found out that on Monday, March 16th, we would no longer have face-to-face classes. The health and wellness program that I am the executive director for needed to shift to virtual courses.

Some people didn't have access and did not know how to use the technology. Being resilient, one of the things that we did and continue to do is reach out every day to maybe ten people. Out of that ten, we were able to get at least one person connected. We then encourage that one person to show someone else how to connect to the training. We used the "each one reach one" approach.

Going virtual for seniors meant someone may fall through the cracks. Thus, undergirding them with extra care to show them how to turn on the sound, how to turn on the visuals, and how to log in was critical. I discovered that the same patience God gave me to use with those science students was still working through me as I helped the seniors get connected with the new technology.

I recognized that if my mother were alive, she would not know how to use the technology either. Neither would she understand all the ramifications of being in a global pandemic. Even though my mother is no longer here, I believe God placed me in the lives of the seniors at the center to coach them through the difficulties. That's a type of resilience and brilliance that comes from facing obstacles. I was reminded that "...tribulation worketh patience; and patience, experience; and experience, hope: and hope maketh not ashamed; because the love of God is shed abroad in our hearts..."[3] I am getting to that perfected place of patience: But it starts with the trouble and the tribulations we face.

The experience at the center helped me realize even more that I am still discovering my purpose as I navigate the ridges in my life successfully. Navigating through those ridges is like mountain climbing. From the bottom, the first thing we think is, "I will never make it to the top." However, once we start the climb and get about midway and look down, we began to tell ourselves, "we can make it to the top if we keep going." As soon as we see the path we traversed,

---

[3]Romans 5: 3-5. *King James Bible*. (2020). King James Bible Online. https://www.kingjamesbibleonline.org

we realize the journey was worth the climb because of the lessons along the way. If we are wise enough to leave markers as we climb, we make that path easier for others coming behind us.

Similarly, my mother's favorite two statements were, "we made it didn't we," and "this too shall pass." Both comments are a testament to her resilience. Life is all about navigation. The word of God has been my compass. I am discovering my purpose daily as I literally seek God's will and surrender to His plan for me.

Even in the toughest of times, such as losing my parents and my beloved sister, Dutchess, I learned never to give up. I have learned to navigate my way to a place of peace with every situation. Lastly, I had to learn to leave out of a difficulty better than I was before I experienced it.

To date, my greatest challenge was continuously struggling to fit in with others. The first time I encountered this problem was being a minority student in all my elementary, middle, and high school classes. The racial divide and racism were blatant. However, not fitting in served me well through the years as I chose the "Road Not Taken," a reference to the narrative poem by Robert Frost published in 1916[4].

> *"...Somewhere ages and ages hence:*
> *Two roads diverged in a wood, and I-*
> *I took the one less traveled by,*
> *And that has made all the difference."*[5]

---

[4] From The Poetry of Robert Frost by Robert Frost, edited by Edward Connery Lathem. Copyright 1916, 1923, 1928, 1930, 1934, 1939, 1947, 1949, © 1969 by Holt Rinehart and Winston, Inc. Copyright 1936, 1942, 1944, 1945, 1947, 1948, 1951, 1953, 1954, © 1956, 1958, 1959, 1961, 1962 by Robert Frost. Copyright © 1962, 1967, 1970 by Leslie Frost Ballantine.

[5] Frost, Ibid.

It was only after attending Alabama A&M University, an HBCU, that I was able to let my guard down and really learn to love myself the way God created me. The historical and cultural experience at Alabama A&M made me proud of who I am, my roots, and the university. The richness of the musical heritage expressed through my professors, Dr. and Mrs. Henry Bradford, caused me not to want to leave Alabama A&M. Their influence continued to motivate me as I worked with the Inspirational Voices Choir at Columbia High School.

For me, that road less traveled made me an educator, counselor, administrator, and mentor for students and teachers for thirty-one years. I drew on my early life experiences to clarify the challenges of working daily with evolving youth.

Many of my former students are now educators, and they tell me they draw on the examples and standards that I set as their former teacher. One of my mentees incurred many challenges as an educator. She faced classroom management problems. I reminded her that classroom management can be problematic for most teachers, so learn to celebrate the wins as much as you lament over the problems. I am also able to share my experiences with our sons, William and Stephen, who are both educators.

I give God all the glory for the resilience that He placed in me to persevere through life's many challenges and then still be relevant, long after I have left that profession and embarked on another.

For anyone shifting from their plans to actively living out their purpose, I desire to share some critical takeaways from my journey.

- Put God first. Seek Him and His plan for your life. His plans are always better than ours.
- Plan a little health and wellness for each day. Don't stop moving. Find someone to walk with you virtually if you can't walk face to face.
- Take each moment and each breath as a gift. Make every day count.
- Open your heart. If you permanently close your heart, nothing goes out, and nothing can come in.
- Learn to give of yourself. Your time, money, expertise, and love have great value in this life when shared with others.
- Forgive quickly. Once a person is gone, it is too late to say, "I'm sorry."
- Don't give up on young people. They have a lot to learn. But, they have even more to teach us.
- Reach out to seniors. If we keep living, we will be one. "Laugh Out Loud (LOL)."
- If you are blessed to be married, please tell your spouse you love them. Always recognize their value. One of my mother's greatest disappointments was that when my dad passed away, she never realized how much she loved him until he was gone.
- Finally, enjoy each day. You are beautiful and marvelously made. Celebrate your life. It is God's desire that we all have life and have it more abundantly.

Dr. Stephanie May is an American Faith Based educator, flautist, songwriter, worship leader and author. For over 40 years, Dr. May has been a member of Bethesda Cathedral of the Apostolic Faith, Inc and she currently serves as the Executive Director of non-profit organization, The Bridge at Austin Community Center.

Dr. May is a retired teacher and administrator in metropolitan Atlanta. She has presented professional learning modules locally and nationally in enlightened content that promotes best practices in science teaching, classroom management and critical thinking. Since retiring, Dr. May has published a series of hymns and worship songs for flute and presented them at local conferences. She serves as a Sunday School teacher at her local assembly in the class, Haven of Strength.

Dr. May is the wife of Robert C. May, her college sweetheart of 42 years. She is the mother of two sons, William and Stephen – both music educators, performers and worshippers.

Contact:
stephanie.may8347@yahoo.com
Web: drmay@thebridgeataustin.org

6

The Triangle of Brillance

Veonicca Wesley

"LIKE THE RUBBER band, I have been able to bounce back while retaining the lessons learned during the stretching process."

Resilience is best described using a rubber band, despite its simple appearance of being JUST a light brown piece of stretchy material. It has so many capabilities. However, its most important characteristic is its ability to stretch. It can be stretched beyond its original shape, but when released, it can return to its original form. My life experiences are very similar to those of the rubber band. Like the rubber band, I have been able to bounce back while retaining the lessons learned during the stretching process. Through these rubber band-like life experiences, my strength has developed through resilience. This resilience has provided me with the capability to achieve and experience brilliance. This visual of a three-part Triangle of Brilliance includes wildness, repentance, and execution.

The Triangle of Brilliance

The term brilliance is not just limited to its definition in a dictionary. Instead, it can be visualized and explained through the usage of a triangle and its tiers. Each of the sides present has a distinct purpose and connects to a different portion of my life. The three sides to be examined are repentance, the wilderness, and execution. Repentance is a time of self-motivation due to the acceptance of past experiences, both good and bad. The wilderness is a place for self-exploration and reflection. It is a time when growth occurs, and God's voice can be distinctly heard within the chaotic world. Then there is execution, where all the lessons, both good and bad, learned in life are combined to fulfill one's purpose. For brilliance to be truly experienced, it is imperative that the individual operates at a high-performance level. This requires the acknowledgment of weaknesses and strengths based on one's life experiences.

To better understand the foundation of brilliance, I have chosen to deconstruct my journey from Alabama and the decision to move to Arizona. I first moved for a summer internship at a Fortune 500 company in 2005 and eventually for full-time employment in 2007 after graduating from Tuskegee University. Not only had I made the decision to move thousands of miles from home for the first summer as an intern. But, I was provided an opportunity to live with my mentor, who is also a pastor, and her family. I was confused. I didn't have a clue of what their expectations would be. Would we be singing hymnals and praying together every morning? It was safe to say I had indeed entered my wilderness. I no longer had parents responsible for me; I was in charge of myself and my destiny.

This self-exploration began as I drove one hour to and from work every day. This time allowed me to reflect on my life and the decisions I made. I also thought about the opportunities, people, and relationships, both positive and negative, that I had encountered. These thoughts covered various areas, such as how I grew up in the church building, but the church or a relationship with God was not genuinely in me. I start thinking about all the friends I lost while on this journey of life. I even asked God, "why am I here in Arizona at this moment?" Inwardly, I heard Him say, "You are here for a purpose. For you to grow, you needed separation from your surroundings and the familiar. You are now in a place where all your grace and strength must come from Me." At these moments, I realized that being thousands of miles from home, driving a total of two hours back and forth from work, and being by myself had purpose. I was truly facing my wildness head-on. During this time, I realized the importance of focusing on and acknowledging my weaknesses during wilderness experiences. But to succeed, it was also necessary to recognize my strengths that were revealed during the stretching process. I bounced back from those weak points, just like the rubber band, as I continued to move forward due to my growth and sincere relationship with God.

The next portion of the brilliance triangle is repentance. As stated previously, it is a time of self-motivation due to the acceptance of past experiences, good or bad. Through careful analysis, I concluded that repentance results from (1) holding on to anger and frustration effortlessly and (2) the inability to forgive. Through the admittance of these characteristics, I was able to work toward eliminating the hurt caused by others to completely heal and free myself.

This timely process of healing occurred through self-motivation such as journaling, writing poems, declarations, and sayings such as, "I've cried myself to sleep for the last time." But more importantly, forgiving others allowed them to eliminate any control they had over my life.

After moving through the side of the triangle called repentance, there is execution. Execution is where lessons, good and bad, are learned in life and combined to fulfill one's purpose. This is the portion of the Brilliance Triangle that is constantly evolving. It is essential to know that an individual will never wholly reach the point of absolute brilliance because there will always be the potential to grow.

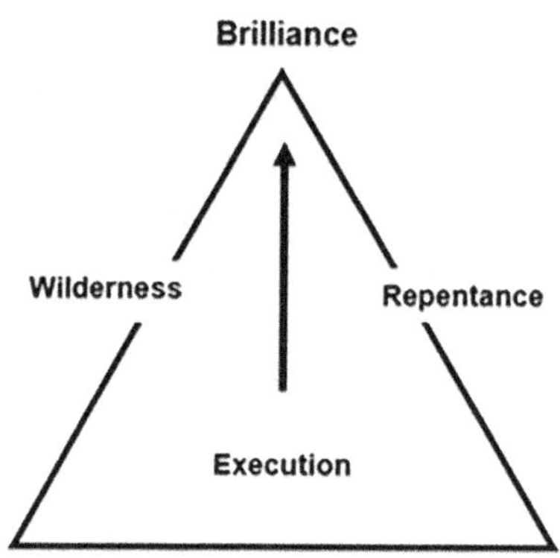

Figure 1: *The Triangle of Brilliance*

Learning to Stretch

The presence of elastic in the rubber band is very significant to its ability to stretch. It determines how far the rubber band is capable of stretching without breaking. On the other hand, if no effort is applied, the rubber band remains in its current form. Therefore, to reach one's full potential, action must be involved. The areas of my life where I encountered stretching is during the period of time where I was forced to have reconstructive ankle surgery. During this time, I learned that today's decisions can impact one's future, either positively or negatively.

This classroom of learning to stretch started as a young girl when I began my journey playing tennis and continued through adolescence. Early on, I found out that I had weak ankles, but my love for tennis and all sports outweighed the pain. Beyond high school, I was accepted as a walk-on for the Varsity Tennis Team at Tuskegee University. The pain increased, and I was told I needed to have reconstructive ankle surgery. I was very stubborn and did not listen. Finally, the pain was unbearable. I stopped playing tennis, but still, I declined to have the surgery.

However, after launching my career in Arizona, I got to the point I could no longer walk without excruciating pain. Surgery was inevitable. I traveled from Arizona back home to Birmingham, Alabama, for the surgical procedure on my left ankle. That experience was twofold. I learned how to survive and overcome an operation that put me in a place of total dependence upon others after tasting success and independence in what I thought was a moment of "living my best life."

Secondly, I had a choice. I could have a pity party or take the higher road and treat the situation as a life-learning experience. Choosing the latter allowed me to rediscover all the people in my life who have always been there for me and willing to lift me up when I was low. I also had time to reflect and reevaluate my positioning relative to the Triangle of Brilliance. I learned I had more strength inside me than I ever thought. I realized that playing sports and involvement in other activities were not my identity.

Another five years passed, and the same surgical procedure was done on my right ankle. Before my upcoming wedding day, I had to wear a boot because of excruciating pain. The surgeon agreed I could wear a shoe instead of an orthopedic boot on my wedding day only if I accepted his timetable for the operation. I complied, and shortly after my wedding, the operation commenced.

During my recuperating time, I gained a new perspective regarding the lives of others. As a leader, I realize that from the surface, it may appear everything is going well for my peers or direct reports. However, unless I demonstrate empathy and put myself in their shoes, I will not discover the depths of the scenarios they are living through.

Some lessons are NOT fun

Another life-learning experience in my early teens also included a sport's related incidence. This lesson occurred because of an association with someone who made a poor, undisciplined decision. Our coach made both of us run in the rain, even though I did not commit the offense. I suffered the consequence, and although the other person stopped running, I accepted my coach's discipline. My mother watched as I ran, and she bolstered my coach's decision even though I told her I did not do anything wrong. Later, in her discussion with me, my mother said, "this life lesson included consequences for your actions." I realized guilt by association is still guilt.

Later in life, as I developed into a leader, this lesson played a significant role. It is a constant reminder that I am responsible for the associations I choose. Other people are watching me. Therefore, my behavior and the choices I make not only affect me but also others. Leadership requires owning the mistakes we make, whether by error or omission. Taking ownership is critical to executing as a leader of an organization and demonstrating brilliance and resilience.

Everyone has a Story

Being the youngest of three girls, I have always grown up in the shadows of my two oldest sisters. Shadows that brought headaches, joy, happiness, burdens, and pain. These different feelings resulted from the struggles to maintain my own identity while overshadowing the expectation set by others as the result of having older siblings. For example, my greatest challenge as the youngest of three children was that I was not the "A" student. I had a spectrum of grades, including "A's, B's, and C's. However, my siblings were brilliant. They were the "A" students. Although my parents never compared us, teachers and others from the outside did. Even people within our local church congregation created moments of comparison that pushed me away from the church. I was told, "you are not as smart as your sisters." I battled with being seen as the lesser of the three children. While the noise from the outside world was overwhelming me, I could draw strength from both of my sisters.

While Keonna has always made every effort to clearly define her motivational tactics, Virnetta utilized a tough-love method that I only understand after we were grown. My understanding of my sister Virnetta occurred after we were both invited to speak at a Girls Inc. Conference in our adulthood. We decided to travel together and even share a hotel room at the conference. During our travels, we had a very candid conversation for the first time. We discussed our differences and exposed the things that divided us all these years. Virnetta thought I was trying to take her place as the older sister. Even though I revealed how I always saw her as a role model, I also shared that I felt she was consistently tough on me. Virnetta's reasoning was that she was driving me to be better. We both realized during our conversation that we were taking each other's actions out of context. The trip and sister dialogue brought healing to our relationship.

My middle sister, who is like a second mom to me, had a different approach. Keonna's arrival at Tuskegee University as an engineering major would motivate me to enroll a year later. We would begin to conquer the goal of being the last two sides of the triangle to obtain an engineering degree. However, this would totally change as Keonna' decided to change her major her junior year after receiving an offer for a professional internship. She decided to utilize the knowledge instilled by our parent's Rodney and Frenetta Greene, that we should always enjoy our profession. She changed her major to History. Upon graduating, she would spend some time at the University of Delaware and eventually work at a law firm. While enjoying this career, she became severely injured in an automobile accident and could no longer work for the law firm. This accident caused her to have severe headaches and forced her to move back in with my parents. Keonna never made excuses regarding her condition. She remained resilient, always saying, "I will learn something from this situation." My sister became a salesperson for a car dealership as she continued to pursue her true passion for becoming a high school history teacher.

Keonna is teaching now, and she loves what she does. She utilizes every step in her Triangle of Brilliance to prepare for this moment. During the COVID-19 pandemic, her experience as a salesperson prepared her for the many telephone calls she needed to make to student's parents while adapting to their various personalities. Compared to all the paperwork required at the law firm, the documentation requirements due to the pandemic were minimal.

Keonna's resilient demeanor, like many others, continues to inspire me. For example, when I received the Black Engineer of the Year Award (BEYA): Professional Achievement Award for the Defense Industry, a few of my family members, including my husband, Clifton, and our daughter, gathered to celebrate. Usually, I am not an emotional person. But when I saw the people in the room, especially Keonna, I shared with them that the award I received was not just because of my achievements. Because of their role modeling and encouragement, I didn't quit my profession as an engineer. Not only was engineering a male-dominated field, I saw firsthand that hard work does bring rewards, including joy and recognition. I remember going to a BEYA Conference over a decade ago while attending Tuskegee University and seeing those brilliant women and men being honored. I also remember thinking, "no one from Birmingham, Alabama will get this opportunity." But it can happen; it happened for me. The sacrifices of the people around me, including my parents, were being rewarded. My father did not go to college, but he made sure his three children had the opportunity. My mother gave up her career to ensure we were taken care of, including all the rides to tennis practice. I had overcome so many obstacles and challenges throughout my life. I, along with my village, was finally recognized.

Living a Brilliant Life

I believe people who strive to live a life of brilliance establish specific guidelines or keys that they follow along the way. The life-learning keys I discovered through my journey in the Triangle of Brilliance include the following:

- Self-awareness is the foundation for discovering who you really are. It means taking off the layers of masks to get to the place of truth, clarification, and peace that only God can give.
- Life-long learning goes beyond the degrees acquired. Therefore, always consider life itself as a school.
- Mentorship means finding a diverse group of mentors who will honestly share their opinions even when they disagree with yours. It is also essential to have mentors who listen without necessarily having to have a voice.
- Communication is vital for execution. To find your brilliance, you must develop critical listening, oratory, and writing skills.
- Goalsetting includes developing a mechanism that will hold you accountable.

I knew I needed a visual that captured the tiers or steps required to meet the goals I set professionally and personally. I used a "One Step Closer" goalsetting document I created based on a challenge from one of my mentors throughout my adult life. I now realize these execution steps depict the tiers of the Triangle of Brilliance concept that has shaped my life.

One vital thought to note is that goals can change over time. According to my "One Step Closer" goals sheet, I wrote I would have a doctorate degree at 31 years old. I did acquire a master's degree, but my life was detoured, and I accepted that changes in my goal setting were needed. I discovered I preferred the Program Management field instead. Therefore, more engineering management training better fits my pursuit. Lily Tomlin said it best, "The road to success is always under construction."[1]

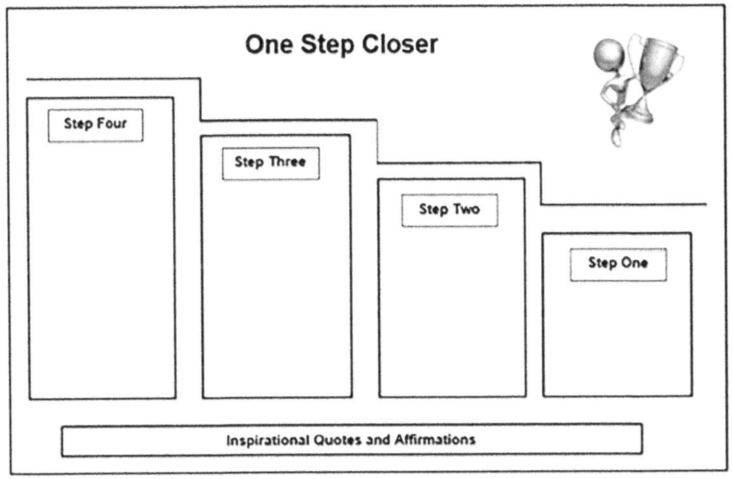

Figure 2 – One Step Closure Chart

According to Denis Waitley, "The secret to productive goal setting is in establishing clearly defined goals and then focusing on them several times a day with words, pictures, and emotions as if we've already achieved them."[2] When setting goals, visualize yourself in that role regardless of

---

[1]Lily Tomlin. website: https://www.lilytomiln.com
[2]Denis Waitley. website: https://www.deniswaitley.com

what others think you can attain. Then, find mentors who are already accomplished relative to that position. Finally, envision the accomplishment from a "finish-start" position. See yourself at the desired destination, and then look back and note what steps it took to get there. From that perspective, the stages of execution are then defined.

Inspirational words and poems have played a vital role in my life. I also include them in my "One Step Closer" goal-setting document. This love for words and inspiration started at an early age as my parents, Rodney and Frenetta Greene, strongly encouraged reading and reciting inspirational poems and quotes. Each day we walked up and down the stairs in our home, skillfully reciting works from poets such as William Hickson, John Greenleaf Whittier, and Robert Frost. As an adult, one of my favorite poems used for motivation is "The Rose that Grew from Concrete" by Tupac Shakar... "Funny it seems, but by keeping its dreams, it learned to breathe fresh air. Long live the rose that grew from concrete when no one else ever cared."[3]

Stop and Smell the Roses

As with many other leaders, the COVID-19 pandemic created a time of self-reflection for me. I took time to review the things I do to reinforce good mental health. Due to the shutdown, I realized I did not have many hobbies or other ways to reduce stress. Basically, my life revolved around our 12-year-old daughter and work. However, during the pandemic, I used walks in the open air to focus on the next phase of my life (retirement); would I teach or coach? I also

---

[3]Tupac Shakur. (2009). *The Rose That Grew From Concrete*. MTV Books: Illustrated edition.

used the downtime to refine my long-term goals. Most importantly, I learned to find beauty in small things.

Additionally, my husband and I noticed we spent more time together as a family during the pandemic than we ever had before. He and I both travel because of our jobs. Before the pandemic, we were home simultaneously, only two weeks out of the month. During this crisis, we took time to deepen our relationship, taking brilliance to new heights. We finally took some time to enjoy some of the things we acquired through our hard work.

I also realized the importance of family and telling people "No" because it is not the right season to seek advancement opportunities. For example, when our daughter was younger, I traveled at a minimum. I knew she needed me more than I needed the career opportunities. I never saw that choice as a hindrance to my career. Instead, I saw it as an investment in our child's life and the chance to reach brilliance as a parent.

Always Under Construction

I believe that our purpose is always under construction. I don't think God reveals our entire purpose all at once. That is why hearing His voice is crucial. It is during those times of navigating and decision-making that purpose is revealed. When we are surrounded by silence, and His calm voice comes over us, or when we reach a breaking point and want to give up, God's voice reminds us we are on this earth for a purpose. Now is not the time to quit. It is during those times; we must stay the course and allow God to navigate our journey. For me, my relationship with God is how I navigate those various ridges in my life to be successful.

During the navigation process, I have learned to include times to celebrate the short-term wins. I noticed that I had not reflected on the successes and short-term wins in my career. I did not take the time to "enjoy the moment," not even a few seconds. There were times I felt I had not accomplished very much. I was looking through the wrong spectrum, watching someone else's successful moments instead of celebrating my own fulfillment of purpose. I have learned to take time to stop and smell the roses. I am definitely an example of the poem "The Rose that Grew from Concrete," by Tupac Sukar. I was able to survive the wilderness in Arizona and move through the places of repentance and eventually upward through the points of execution, the Triangle of Brilliance.

Through the appreciation and guidance of individuals from my past and present, I have learned to use my negative and positive experiences to motivate myself and others. I thanked all my teachers who told me "I couldn't" because their words inspired me to work harder and achieve more. It is also for one of my friends that passed away. Their last words to me were, "V, don't ever change." Me taking the time to smell the roses was for my husband as well. He is my biggest cheerleader. Finally, it is for my grandmother, Mrs. Margaret T. White, who allows me to stand on her shoulders along with the shoulders of my ancestors that led the way before me. This time of reflection is very humbling.

I am thankful for the opportunity to mentor others and help them become more resilient on their roads to success. I use the word, roads because I realize each mentee's journey through the tiers of the triangle to brilliance is different. Additionally, I recognize the importance of listening and quietly praying behind the scenes as a mentor. There should not be any selfish motives when mentoring. I give to organizations and help others without questions if I feel led by God to do so. Giving time to others through teaching and mentoring is a critical component of my success journey.

Critical takeaways for shifting from plans to purpose include the following:

- Remain true to yourself.
- Resilience is the model to brilliance.
- Write your plan and execute it.

Pursue your purpose, the reason why you are on the earth.

Finally, I end this chapter with an excerpt from one of the poets my parents introduced me to while climbing the stairs in our home.

When things go wrong as they sometimes will,
When the road you're trudging seems all up hill,
When the funds are low and the debts are high
And you want to smile, but you have to sigh,
When care is pressing you down a bit,
Rest if you must, but don't you quit...[4]

---

[4]John Greenleaf Whittier. "Don't Quit."

Veonicca Wesley is a native of Birmingham, Alabama. She is the youngest of three children born to Rodney and Frenetta Greene. Wesley has been working in the defense industry for over 15 years. She is a wife and mother of one daughter. Her passion includes mentoring high school and college students. In her spare time, she enjoys cooking, reading, and performing community service

Wesley has a Master of Science in Engineering Management from California University, Northridge and a Bachelor of Science in Mechanical Engineering from Tuskegee University. She has successfully earned the following awards and certifications. She is a Level 6 Program Manager, Six Sigma Specialist, Department of the Army Certificate of Completion Javelin Field Training Course (Gunner Training), and Team Achievement Awards for her ongoing commitment to outstanding performance.

Contact:
veoniccawesley@yahoo.com

7

The Journey to Brilliance

Rukiya Higgins

BRILLIANCE, TO ME in an untraditional sense, is the culmination of our life experiences, journeys, and revelations that act as a tool to uncover the proverbial gem within to reveal the authentic you. In similarity to a chisel, our lived experiences slowly reveal the core of who we are by the applied pressure of life and, at the right time, expose the beauty beneath in the form of our shine. So, the purpose of the chisel is to illuminate – it is to cut away the unwanted, carve a new pathway, and reveal the essence of a thing. And the intersectionality of these experiences allows you to fully embrace your brilliance – your best self, as a person.

So, let's start at the beginning. My name, Rukiya, is Swahili for "She Rises High." For me, my name is not only a descriptor but a calling that identifies. I was raised in the inner city of Detroit, the birthplace of Motown Records, where some of the greatest hits were produced. Also nicknamed the Motor City, Detroit is the historic heart of the automotive industry and the home of the Detroit Windsor Tunnel, which is the first traffic tunnel built between nations. But while all these statements are true, Detroit was also once considered the "Murder Capital" of the world. So, I navigated this world of history and harshness, and from an early age, I learned resilience and how it was important for me to rise above my circumstances even amid chaos.

To fully embrace my story of resilience, we must start at a pivotal point in my journey – transitioning to high school. As a youngster full of promise, I had my heart set on attending one of the top high schools in the city known for graduating the best and the brightest. This school had a remarkably high success rate of students pursuing advanced degrees at universities and colleges all over the nation. I worked hard and envisioned myself following this path, but to my surprise, I was redirected. My redirection was due to the competitiveness of the school applicants, and I was not accepted. In parallel, though, I was pursued and recruited by another high school that touted their exceptional advanced program for high potential students though it had a reputation for gang violence and poverty. Initially, it felt like second best but little did I know, over 4 years, (30) thirty of us students would be cocooned in a specialized program meant to advance us to opportunities that would expand our horizons.

After graduating from high school, I left Detroit for a different world, both figuratively and literally. In the 80s, there was a show called A Different World, which was a spin-off from The Cosby Show that highlighted collegiate life at a fictional HBCU (Historically Black College and University). That show gave me permission to believe that college was attainable. If the African American characters could pursue professional degrees, then so could I, hence the reason I decided to attend

Tuskegee University. Now imagine leaving everything you know – your family, your friends, your comfortability for the unknown. It was not easy. As a matter of fact, it was a huge culture shock to move from the fast-paced city of Detroit to the slow-paced countryside of Tuskegee, but that experience changed the trajectory of my life. It allowed me to expand my outlook to formulate long-lasting friendships and learn in an emotionally safe environment. As a result, I obtained a bachelor's degree in Mechanical Engineering and, years later, the confidence to pursue a master's degree in Engineering Science from Rensselaer Polytechnic Institute.

Fast forward to the present, I am an Engineering professional with an array of experience across a broad spectrum of industries. My career has morphed into the best of both the technical and business worlds to give me a well-rounded portfolio of experience. However, my expectation of how my career journey was supposed to take shape did not happen. As I took on roles of progressive leadership and responsibility – promotional opportunities lagged, so stretch assignments, lateral positions, special projects as they were called were becoming the norm and difficult at times to embrace. But what I learned early in life was to bounce back quickly, maximize on the opportunity at hand and continue to prepare in the "in-between" time because at the purposed time, when my preparation and opportunity meet, it would produce success.

Through difficulties, challenges, and roadblocks, I developed fortitude. It was critical to have these occasions to overcome obstacles because they built character and integrity. The combined effort to intentionally focus and continue to strive helped me to maximize my potential. Over time, I realized the brilliance inside of me, which I discovered like a precious gem, layer by layer, until I was able to appreciate my uniqueness aligned to my purpose.

Reinventing Ourselves through Crises

The COVID-19 pandemic has been a once in a lifetime opportunity for reinvention. For many, including myself, life changed dramatically from daily commutes to telecommuting, social interactions to social distancing, freedom to restrictions, but being able to quickly switch directions and accept the reality of the new norm was key. I decided I did not want to exit the pandemic the same as I entered. I wanted to find a way to emerge stronger, smarter, and more prepared. So, I took advantage of the extra time within quarantine to cultivate my gifts, mature my professional skills and be intentional about self-care.

Long before the pandemic, I decided I needed to set a goal to learn something new and do something that scared me yearly. For three years, I did bodybuilding and competed locally. Initially, the choice to body build was twofold, #1 – I wanted to become a healthier version of myself, and #2 – I admired people's physique in that sport. As I progressed toward this goal, setbacks could have derailed my plan to step on stage, ranging from training fatigue, accurately tracking food consumption, and balancing work commitments that included travel while maintaining the strict discipline required to ultimately achieve. Giving up was not an option; however, it could have easily happened without clear and SMART™ (Specific, Measurable, Achievable, Results-Based, and Timely) goals. But I did it, not once, but three times! In the end, I learned that physical strength was just as crucial as mental toughness.

Another opportunity to learn something new was through music. I love the musicality of the piano, so I learned to play.

I've always loved piano and found it mesmerizing when someone had the ability to master the keys to make beautiful sounds; however, I was intimidated by the grandness of the instrument. I already had an appreciation for music because I played the violin but learning to read and play in bass clef was overwhelming. So, I took lessons for one year and, although still a novice, I enjoyed the fullness and beauty of the piano.

Public speaking – who loves it? Not me! I have never been keen on purposely finding opportunities to speak because although it wasn't new, it was scary. Interestingly enough, speaking found me. I started feeling compelled to share my story, but not just any story, my STEM (Science, Technology, Engineering, and Mathematics) story. This led me to opportunities to speak to a range of audiences from elementary school through college to early career professionals at various conferences, corporate-sponsored community events, and non-profit organizations. These opportunities collectively helped me realize that I have a natural ability to motivate, inspire and connect with the younger generation. So, I joined Toastmasters to develop that muscle and refine this skill. It became clear that another layer had chiseled away, revealing more of who I am and what I was purposed to do. My responsibility was to honor the gift, develop it and share it.

Discovering my best strengths happened when I persevered through the unknown. We develop and strengthen parts of ourselves that lay dormant when we're forced out of our comfort zone. A lot of times, we spend time in the safe zone in the sureness of our abilities. We run in the opposite direction of anything that could cause us to fail, but it is in those times that the real chiseling begins. We all have talents and strengths, but if left under-developed, it becomes a missed opportunity to see that gift evolve within the sphere of our influence. Stretching and growing beyond our fears is imperative. My stance is to do the thing we fear – just do it scared! I found that we grow the most when we strive toward the things that challenge us the most. Be mindful; resilience requires being uncomfortable sometimes – doing things that may be daunting. However, the journey to purpose is a process, and we are responsible for uncovering it.

I remember struggling to figure out my purpose, but I had an epiphany. I realized I had been living and cultivating my purpose all along. Maybe I expected a grand reveal of my life's mission, but my purpose was the things I gave space to every day. Those things included the professional leadership journey I worked hard to pursue, investing my time in the community to develop the next generation of leaders, speaking to motivate and inspire, and appreciating the things that gave me joy. My purpose confirmed itself through personal relationships, my achievements, and the things I naturally gravitated to that brought me joy.

As I realized my purpose, one of my most significant challenges was overcoming imposter syndrome. Well into my career journey, I still struggled with feeling like a fraud and that someone would discover that perhaps I wasn't deserving enough to be doing the things I was doing or intelligent enough to be invited into the spaces I was invited to. Although I have many accomplishments, advanced degrees, I felt I just wasn't enough. I allowed fear to tell me that someone would realize I should not be there, and it gripped me. For instance, in meetings, I would sit on the outskirts of a conference room in hopes that I would blend into the wall. I did not want to sit at the table because I was intimidated by the perceived intelligence of everyone else. I had something to contribute, but I was unsure of myself, so I hid. I hid until an executive leader gave me some validating advice. She said, "Never go into a room you are invited to and downplay your presence. You were invited for a reason, so you deserve to be there. Sit at the table and always be prepared to contribute." That was the start of accepting my position in life and doing so authentically.

Inspired by a Matriarch

Inspiration for me comes through various influences like family, community, culture, art, travel, and music, which have been some of my greatest teachers. But of all the teachers, my maternal grandmother and mother have been the most influential. These two women taught me how to become the woman I am today. They are my examples of resilience and how to thrive in a world that was not scripted for their success. My mother's ingenuity to create opportunities within an environment that seemingly had nothing to offer; took forethought and perceptiveness. She provided an avenue for my sibling and me to explore through the lens of books, art, and music. My mother encouraged us to expand our way of thinking by reading, understanding the significance of art, and appreciating music. Growing up, we spent many Saturdays at the Detroit Public Library reading books, encyclopedias, newspapers, and it became a fun place for us to learn in the city. Likewise, we spent a great deal of time enjoying various art exhibits at the Detroit Institute of Arts, and from time to time, even traveling exhibits. It was an inexpensive way to expose and immerse us in culturally rich experiences enabling us to dream, teaching us different perspectives, to prepare us for the world in front of us. Also, living in a city with a rich heritage of music, we found appreciation in the likes of Gospel music – the heart of the black church, Rhythm and Blues that resided in the heart of the city, as well as Jazz that brought a fusion of sound that penetrated the soul. By all accounts, we were a family of little means, but my mother relied on her inner strength and tenacity to provide her children with a well-rounded wealth of knowledge.

My grandmother was a spirited woman! She was a witty intellectual, savvy entrepreneur, and fashionista. My grandma was an influencer in her own right by how she carried herself no matter the struggle that lay ahead. She was always prepared. Prepared to converse with the likes of dignitaries, neighbors, family, and anyone who enjoyed conversating because she prided herself in staying connected not only with what was going on in society – in culture but in common folk's lives, including her grandchildren. She was a voracious reader that read the newspaper daily, fashion magazines like Harper's Bazaar and the W, and premier publications for African Americans such as Ebony, Jet, and the Michigan Chronicle. She was also a contemplator who listened to the news and other happenings on the radio, so when the time came to socialize and conversate, she always had something to talk about. In her days of being a Domestic, she traveled by city bus to her job for 20 years to support her family, all while sharing the responsibilities of operating as a landlord with my grandfather to supplement their household income. But at the most impressionable time in my life, I observed how my grandma presented herself. She took care to look her best everywhere she went. Dressed head to toe, you noticed Mrs. Flemings – fingernails polished, makeup just right, hair neat with a fashionable outfit, and a pair of her favorite 3-inch-high heels. No one did it better than my grandmother. She was the example of how to hold your head up high and live your best life with the cards you are dealt. I learned how to walk tall with confidence by watching how my grandmother did it.

A Heritage of Resilience

My ancestors are the most resilient people I have never met. They were the hard workers, who had unconventional smarts, mental and physical toughness, entrepreneurial astuteness, intuitive leadership, and these are the characteristics that were passed down to me. I am not resilient because I am unique. I am resilient because it is in my blood. So many of my great-great aunts, uncles, cousins passed through this land before me that paved the way, so I stand on the shoulders and in the shadows of all of those that created the opportunities I have today. One of those greats is my great-grandfather. He was a businessman that specialized in plaster contracting. He traveled around the nation as a builder and built a family home where my grandmother was raised. In the 1900s, owning a home in suburban Detroit meant you were a person of prominence, but my family shattered that stereotype. So, when I reflect on my family lineage, it makes me proud of the strength and courage they possessed and passed along to me.

The collective lessons I garnered from my mother and grandmother, my ancestors, and my community helped shape how I have chosen to approach my life to discover my best self. Some of those lessons are:

- Difficulties, challenges, and roadblocks are necessary to help you develop resilience.
- Being your authentic self provides you the freedom to be the best you.
- Your purpose will confirm itself through the things you naturally gravitate toward.

- When you are forced out of your comfort zone, you develop and strengthen parts of yourself that lay dormant.
- Don't be afraid to do things that intimidate you because it may reveal something about yourself you didn't know was there.
- A good indicator that you are on the road to discovering who you are meant to be is you continue to strive.
- Every day you are living your purposed legacy.

Building the Muscle of Resilience

Resiliency has been a muscle I have developed over time through unwanted disappointments, obstacles, and redirections because I developed emotional maturity, forged alternate pathways to success, and continued to invest in my personal development.

Developing emotional maturity took effort because it was learning how to manage my feelings and reactions appropriately. There have been many times through various phases of my life when I blamed other people and circumstances for the demise of a relationship, an unsuccessfully executed project, or missed opportunities because I did not want to take responsibility for my contribution to something that went wrong. It was easier to place blame because it made me feel better; however, in not taking responsibility, I had less control of my emotions. A quote by an unknown author that I think is important to ponder says, "Our emotions need to be as educated as our intellect. It is important to know how to feel, how to respond, and how to let life in so that it can touch you." So, over time, I learned how to accept, correct, and move forward from disappointment maturely, which leads me to forge alternate pathways to success.

Life offers many options. We start on one path and end on another by the choices we make. Similarly, when a path isn't leading to the planned destination that you intended, it's up to you to make a change. Consequently, I've learned the art of the pivot. Reflecting on when I worked for a company that was going through a reorganization – short for downsizing their workforce, I remember rethinking my career journey at that company. During this time, I was extremely concerned that I would be part of the staff reduction, so I decided that it was in my best interest to secure another opportunity elsewhere. Honestly, it was inconvenient and a bit scary to pursue other opportunities because I was comfortable. I was in a comfort zone because, in addition to the work being satisfying, I was surrounded by family, longtime friends, and a community of support. However, in the end, I decided to make a change and take a chance. I opened myself to the possibility of relocating and switching industries, which was one of the best decisions I have ever made personally and professionally. At that time, I had a choice – I could have remained content and concerned about my job stability or create a different path. I choose the latter, and I am better for it.

Lastly, to maximize on new opportunities, it is also important to consider personal development. When I learn new things, I feel empowered because it makes me better as an individual. As an example, in a professional capacity, it is essential that I cultivate my business acumen skills as I progress in my career. The good thing is those skills are transferable outside of the workplace. I can utilize those skills to manage my personal finances, make strategic investment decisions and personal relationships. Just like learning a new sport such as tennis, which requires flexibility, agility, and persistence, in the same way, career progression does as well, so I can leverage these skills to be a better employee. So, personal development is not narrowly focused on one area of your life; it adds value to you as a total person.

Discovering Our Resilience

I have had the opportunity to help others navigate their own road to resiliency by sharing lessons I've learned that have been used as a roadmap of sorts. The biggest lesson is to never give up because, in the end, you will always uncover things about yourself you didn't even realize were there, and eventually, success finds you. Success may not look like what you expected, but it is success, nonetheless. The realization is that we all experience setbacks and roadblocks as we are discovering our best selves, but it is how we respond in those times and what we do going forward that are the best indicators of success. Sometimes, we are so eager to progress through life to meet our lifelong goals quickly that we miss the importance of what life is all about. We are meant to grow and progress in stages to contribute something special at every juncture of our life.

Life is the chisel that exposes our purpose and the brilliance within us, so we must embrace and cultivate all that is revealed. My story is still being written, and in the middle of this journey, I choose to continue to evolve and allow the layers of myself to be exposed. I want to ensure that my purposed legacy impacts the generations to come, and that happens by intentionally making the most of every opportunity. She Rises High is my calling, and as I persist along this journey, that is exactly what I intend to do.

Rukiya Higgins is an accomplished leader with over 22 years of experience in the Aerospace/Defense and Automotive Industries. She has had roles of progressive leadership that has given her significant depth and breadth of knowledge in Engineering, Operations, Supply Chain, IT and Program Management. Rukiya's career has been marked by many achievements, recognitions and opportunities that are a demonstration of her proven success.

Additionally, Rukiya is passionate about motivating and uplifting the younger generation to strive for excellence in their educational pursuits as they successfully transition from academia to the workplace. Rukiya earned her Master of Science in Engineering Science from Rensselaer Polytechnic Institute and Bachelor of Science in Mechanical Engineering from Tuskegee University.

Contact Information:
Website: www.rukiyahiggins.com
Email: contact@rukiyahiggins.com

8

Resilience is Built Through Living Life

Sonya Drayer

THE CREATIVE ENERGY brought to an event or life situation represents our inner brilliance when operating from a place and space within our inner genius. That creative energy varies from person to person and occurs based on how we live our life. The revelation of my inner genius occurred when I entered the marketplace after college. Through my progression and growth in my career, my confidence level has grown, and my passion for learning continues to increase. During my career, I have had the opportunity to participate in various roles and rotational programs offered by employers I have worked for. I learned different skills, and I was excited and stimulated, allowing my creative energy to flow. The rotations consisted of six to twelve months in various functions with completion deadlines for special projects on each rotation. I engaged in the projects by asking the right questions, offering solutions, and then putting the pieces together, demonstrating my inner genius. What I didn't realize at the time was how I was building my resilience muscle. When you have to switch teams and sometimes locations every six to twelve months, you have to learn to be comfortable being the new person often. I was put into roles and situations I had little to no experience in and had to figure out how to take the skills and experiences I did have and get really good at starting over and making an impact in a short period of time.

Accepting new challenges is an optimal way to gain experience and grow. However, it takes courage to step out of our comfort zones and sometimes we are more hesitant than others to take those steps. Oftentimes, these moments of experimenting lead to building our resilience to solve challenges or problems, whether working for ourselves as an entrepreneur or someone else. This process prepares us for the future we have not yet realized and the beginning of building blocks to being resilient.

Resilience is also developed when we pivot and choose a different option because we experienced a failure such as losing or changing jobs, divorce or ending a relationship, etc. These failures can produce greater resilience because we set our will and make a decision to keep trying. If we embrace these moments when failures occur or when the results don't happen as planned, we build resilience muscles instead of running from the discomfort. I have experienced what I perceived as failures in my life. When this happens, I take the time to assess the situation and note the things within my control to change. Questions asked include: "Could I have collaborated more to come up with greater innovative solutions?" or "What do I want the future to look like based on what happened?" Many times, following a failure or misstep, what I find is that I learned, developed, or strengthened an aspect of myself that I had not focused on in the past or would otherwise be unaware needed sharpening. I have found that I generally follow a process of reflection with setbacks. My process consists of the following:

- I **acknowledge or identify** the failure or misstep. "What happened?"
- I **reflect** on the situation to determine how it made me feel.
- I **analyze and seek to understand** what caused the failure or misstep.
- I **ascertain the lessons** learned from the failure or misstep.
- I **identify areas of growth** that are needed moving forward.

During the reflection process, I also study my system, noting any habits, good or bad, that may have contributed to the problem. I ask myself, "Was it a lack of patience that brought me to this point, or did I move too slow?" Other reflective questions include, "Did I under or overthink the process?" or "Did I shy away from the opportunity because of fear of failure or success?" or "Should I have sought advice or input?" Throughout the reflection process regarding my habits, I may discover I have strengths I can use next time or that served me well during this episode. I may also identify weaknesses or tendencies about myself that need shoring up. In the end, maturity has been developed if I can learn from it.

Inspired Resilience

My parents are my biggest cheerleaders and inspire me from where they came from and how they provided for my siblings and me. They worked hard and helped others along the way as they came up. I remember them modeling the behavior of opening our home to family to help them get started in their life's journey or careers. Something I have done in my own home as an adult. I was fortunate enough to have both parents in the home growing up. My parents were actively involved and present for all of my school events and extracurricular activities. If sports were the activity, they supported my games in and out of town. My parents also motivated me to excel in academics, pointing out my brilliance regardless of the circumstances and always pushing me to excellence. Whenever I doubted myself, they were there to cheer me on, encourage me to work hard, and brag about how smart I was. Yeah, I know, most parents say that about their kids. For me, those words empowered me; they made me believe in myself that I could do *ANYTHING*. What I didn't realize then, but appreciate now, is how they spoke life and belief in my abilities. Positive words spoken over your children, or anyone for that matter, can plant seeds of resilience that can manifest themselves at just the right time or season for encouragement. We should work to always lift others up with words of encouragement. You never know when someone is going through something, and your words are just what they need to hear, to keep pushing through and borrow your belief in themselves for that moment.

I am inspired by the authors of self-development books related to the mind and mindset. I found that the more I study the awesomeness of the mind, the more in awe I am of God, our Creator. I have made an intentional effort to reflect on and be more conscious of my thoughts and what I allow my mind to focus on or what thoughts I allow to dwell there. What I discovered through my readings is how powerful thoughts, mindset and the words we speak are. This is reminiscent of the words spoken over me by my parents. These thoughts shape our beliefs, and these beliefs become our reality. Once I grasped that concept and was intentional about my mindset, I realized how powerful I can be and what already exists inside of me. I continually work to re-align and be conscious of how I speak and think about myself. This also affects how we respond to life's challenges. If I constantly have the mindset that I will get through any challenge and trust that the answers to any problem will come, I can handle and be anything I want to be. It's like having a superpower.

When I am discouraged, or experience doubts about my capabilities, I remind myself of God's inspired thoughts toward me and who I am because of Him. When those little creeping voices try to enter my head and tell me that I can't do something, I refresh my mind with what the scripture says about me and remember all of the times I made it through life's challenges. Those actions remind and inspire me that I have a purpose on this earth. I am also reminded that my personality, interests, and talents are important in God's eyes. Each of us is unique. Only YOU can bring to the world that gift and that thing that YOU do, the way YOU do it. So don't ever give up on yourself or cultivating those gifts. The world needs YOU.

Finally, I have been inspired by a group of women and single moms in my life. I realized these were some of the most resilient people I know. I am also a single mom, and we encourage each other and build one another up. As single moms, when our children depend on us, we become resourceful, finding the means to make "something out of nothing." Single parenthood requires mental toughness. Don't get me wrong, there are sometimes meltdowns, lots of prayer, and the need for occasional girl time to remind yourself you are not crazy and not alone. Single parents know there often isn't time to not be resilient. I often reflect on when my son was younger, and I had sole responsibility of his day-to-day activities and rearing. I remember always thinking, I don't have time to be sick because he still needed to eat or attend extracurricular activities. Often times there wasn't anyone else to pick up the slack; I had to make it happen.

Being a single mom and watching these other single mothers, I noticed a pattern of resilience.

- Resilient single moms stop making excuses and just get it done.
- Resilient single moms may have moments of wanting to break down, but they rise to the occasion.
- Resilient single moms know how to be creative and stretch their time and their resources.
- Resilient single moms reframe the situation by not thinking, "I can't do this," but changing their thoughts to "How can I get this done?"
- Resilient single moms change patterns of behavior that are not serving them. These women ensure they have the appropriate people surrounding them to make a better life for their children and themselves. They develop a support network to help fill in the gaps as needed.

- Resilient single moms know how to change the trajectory, providing their children with greater opportunities than they had in life.
- Resilient single moms set goals expecting to accomplish them. They navigate through the situations, doing what is necessary to make it happen.

Developing Keys to Brilliance

Like these women I described, I do not allow the "victim mentality" to enter my thoughts. When I got divorced, I knew there was no power in a "victim mentality." This mentality keeps us from growing and allowing the world to see the inner gifts and talents we received at birth. To overcome the "victim mentality," strategize from a place of power to move forward and show up daily as the victor and design your future.

I have used online platforms, social media, college, videos, and whatever I could find available to develop a skill and find the brilliance within. There are several writers, YouTubers, and other business owners I have followed and learned from. These are my informal mentors. However, don't just depend on them. You can find a real-life mentor who has mastered the skill you want to develop and learn from them as well. Apply the knowledge gained and put in the consistent work necessary to develop further. I also use authors of books to serve as mentors, enlightening me in areas that need further development. We should be creative to get information from people that inspire us.

Remember, the power of the creativity needed to solve any problem or move us forward is already within us. That power is just waiting to be cultivated and nurtured through experience and practice, which causes it to rise to the surface at the right time. You have to experiment and not be afraid to try new things. Don't be afraid to fail, and do not choose only the things you know you will be great at; this is key. The risk and the reward could be found in trying something new when you don't know for sure you will succeed.

Finally, our purpose could be what we are naturally drawn to or what others seek out about us. You should meditate on finding out and seeking what this is. Asking the people in our circle of influence about those characteristics and reflecting on our passions related to an idea or circumstance may lead us to our purpose. Once discovered, we should strengthen our expertise in that area. Even though we have busy lives, we need to take the time to reflect on and clearly define our purpose and the brilliance on the inside of us waiting to be unleashed. When we do not take the time to define our purpose and the brilliance within us, we are doing a disservice to the world and ourselves. There are people in need of what we have or can bring to the table. God placed us on this earth for a specific reason, and we need to make ourselves available to accomplish that purpose.

Resilience through Crisis

Most people will reflect on 2020 with a different lens based on their experiences. The racial injustices brought to the center stage in America, the job losses, the economy, the lives lost to Covid, and the fact that we were wearing masks to protect ourselves reflected the need for resilience in the year 2020. It was an exhausting year that set off many emotional triggers through the media, relationships, and other social platforms.

I was fortunate to maintain my job and work from home during the COVID-19 pandemic. However, pivoting to remote work while dealing with emotional trauma created moments where resilience was required because we still had to show up and get the job done. I relied on those resilient patterns developed as a single mom and kept pushing my way through trauma and anxiety. That didn't mean I didn't acknowledge the exhaustion from the emotions. I found a way to take some breaks, dig deep and carve out a new normal.

Even though 2020 was a challenging year, I spent time reflecting on what I really want in life. I took the time to fast, pray, be still and focus on how I wanted to move forward, how can I move forward, and what is really important to me. I decided I was adding resilience to my list of strengths. The fact that we made it through 2020 demonstrated that we are resilient. I reflected on hard times and challenges from my past, remembering that I made it through them, which laid the foundation for making it through 2020 and beyond in the same manner. Although I was stretched physically and emotionally during this time, I still took time to pause and rest because we were quarantined. I took advantage of the "shut down" by reading more to learn about things that aroused my curiosity that I never had time to study out before. After joining a Facebook group, I took time to create by remodeling an outdoor space at my home as a DIY (do it yourself) project. Completing this project gave me a space to enjoy the outside and do something I had not done before. I created a retreat for my family.

During this time, I also thought about how I want to help others explore and discover their gifts, sharing some of the information I absorbed during the pandemic. Taking the time for self-discovery, I evaluated what was working for me and those things not working to serve my higher self. I also noted the things that are holding me back. I felt like I was lost in a monotonous routine and needed something more.

I decided to prioritize myself in the first quarter of 2021. I have been a "people pleaser" by nature most of my life, putting others' needs and requests before my own. I focused on understanding that pattern and how it left me no time for trying the new things I wanted for myself. I wanted more time to encourage others and figure out how I could inspire others. I needed to work on setting better boundaries and evaluating how I spent my resources. Because it was so easy to say yes to everything, I had to learn when it was okay to say no, that's not right for me, or not right now. I didn't have the discipline I needed to manage my time, which required managing myself and the things I signed up for. This was a habit I needed to refine. I also identified other habits I needed to develop and to strengthen my skills in.

I discovered I needed to grow more in self-discipline. I set a goal to read more consistently. I read more than 30 books during the 2020 shutdown. I developed a consistent exercise regimen that inspired me while building confidence that I can develop healthy habits. This form of self-discipline, reading and exercising, poured into other areas of my life. I learned the importance of exercise and nutrition and their impact on our brains, discovering that these two things are the fundamental keys to success and growth. Not focusing on healthy living and exercise could limit our success. I shared some of this information with my friends, and I was amazed to see the benefits they gained when they incorporated the same knowledge into their lives. We were able to encourage each other and grow together while rewarding ourselves because of our achievements.

Navigating the Ridges to Find Purpose

Navigating is a continuous process in discovering purpose. Self-discovery and knowing thyself coincides with navigating, which led me to research my enneagram type, a form of personality test. I realized I had some conditioning and patterns of fear that hindered me from pursuing specific opportunities. When faced with those fears, it was essential to understand the triggers that cause such insecurities. Navigating and learning to move despite my fears allows me to make more deliberate choices that make way for my future. It gives me the awareness of when to be bold and when to exercise faith and perseverance to not give up. I don't always eliminate some fears; I learn to recognize the feeling and emotions behind them and use different tools to push through them. Navigating through the ridges helped me to determine the career roles I enjoy and those I do not. I am now working on making decisions on what I want to do, rather than holding back based on fear of failure.

While discovering your purpose, it is wise to have a core group of friends who hold you accountable and serve as your council or board of directors. Feedback from them is crucial as you navigate the ridges to success. You have to define your purpose, construct a plan to achieve it, and put it into action. These trusted advisors will help to hold you accountable for executing that plan. Others from the outside may not perceive what those close to you can see. They know when you are not pushing yourself and that you are capable of more than what you believe. They are like a trainer or coach that requires those extra ten squats when you don't feel like you have anything else in you. My friends have commented that I can be encouraging and how I am a skilled organizer. I took this input and meditated on where this shows up in my life and career and is it really true.

I discovered that I enjoy taking data, analyzing it, and placing it into a meaningful process that can be developed into a system. As a Supplier Engineer, my career responsibilities place me at the startup of a new product or process with a supplier or where there is a problem. I take the data and other information generated and organize it to resolve the issue and develop a way forward. That data may include what is not working and what additional help may be needed. I oftentimes can see the vision, the steps, and the resources needed to get there. At times, I need resources to execute the vision. I then lay out a new schedule with milestones, allowing for status reports and organized meetings that navigate us to the finish line. I love order and process; chaos drives me crazy. My gifting shows up in me at work every day, bringing order in chaos while encouraging those around me and being willing to help out when I can.

Recognizing Challenges and Turning them into an Advantage

One of my most significant challenges was facing divorce. I realize all divorces are not equal, and everyone's situation is unique. As I went through the process, for me, it was like the loss of a loved one to death. However, that person is still walking around with a new or different life from the one built together as a couple expecting a "happily ever after." I had to learn how to interact with my former spouse healthily for the sake of our son. The issues we had in the marriage did not go away either, which confirmed why we were better not together. There were hurt feelings and anger to overcome. The challenge was figuring out how to get beyond those emotions and the disappointments regarding the life I thought I would have in order to co-parent in a positive way that was conducive to the well-being of our son.

Another challenge in this situation was knowing that although I grew up in a two-parent home, our son would not have that chance. I had to find our new normal. My friends and church family helped me through that challenge, and I discovered the resilience within me at that point in my life. I chose not to remain stuck in those emotions, and I kept moving forward.

I decided my son and I would make new memories and discover life together. He got involved in various sports, developing new friendships while getting exercise and having fun. When he was younger, we had a family gym membership that included youth activities and a dining area, giving us more chances for a fun, healthy outlet. We also traveled to different countries, going on cruises and making new memories with another single mom and her children. I realize that not every mom can afford to do some of the things I shared. However, making new memories is key to moving beyond the challenge.

Another challenge was work-life balance as a single parent and career-minded woman. I navigated getting my son to and from school and other activities. I also had to travel at times for work. My family and friends helped me during that time. I found safe, reliable friends to become roommates, to live with us. They served as caretakers or chauffeurs when I could not be there for him. Sometimes having roommates was challenging, but there were benefits like them serving as a second mom when needed.

There were times we shared game nights, had cookouts, and hosted other singles in our home, creating a family-type atmosphere. Our house gained a nickname called "The Ridge." My son enjoyed the engagement with other friends and families. These new memories and opportunities to connect with new families came through the difficulty of a divorce. I had the choice to embrace the challenge, make the best of it, and move forward.

Helping Others Move Forward

Since I read so much, I share the knowledge I gain with anyone who will listen or seek self-development input. My passion is to encourage women to fulfill their purpose. I share my experiences of divorce to help other moms who are facing similar circumstances realize they can make it through the challenge. I also encourage them to view their situations differently instead of focusing on their current state.

I help cheer other single moms and women on to explore and celebrate their gifts and talents. I also help these women celebrate the space in life they are currently in, making good decisions for themselves and their children in their single lifestyle. I encourage women to pursue their dreams, knowing that all it takes is creating a plan, focus, and hard work. Sometimes you need the help of a coach to help you formulate a plan. Maybe this is the purpose I spoke of before that I discovered. Stay tuned....

Remember, we have access to divine wisdom and creativity. When we acknowledge we have access to God's wisdom, our potential becomes unlimited. We can start dreaming about crafting our future. Therefore, the thoughts we have and perpetuate about ourselves are critical. I read that we attract who we are, meaning self-revelation is vital. We can start by having the right belief system about ourselves. We should spend time in self-reflection to know who we really are, and the talents, gifts, and passion implanted in us, and then believe in them. So much so, that you can feel it, walk in it and be it. Don't get stuck in the wrong mindset about yourself; there is a higher version of you, waiting to be released.

Sometimes it may seem overwhelming to think about our future when we are in a trial. But remember that each decision, thought, and step we take leads us to our future. The thoughts and intentions that we had months or years ago show up today in our current life circumstances. Those decisions we made brought us to this point. Therefore, we must make wise choices and change the conditioning of our thinking for crafting our future. Always know that we can create a different path and change our trajectory for our future. You have to keep moving forward.

My challenge to you; what is the one thing you can do to construct and devise a plan to move forward? Start small and be sure to write it down or journal your answers. If you make small, consistent steps towards this plan, your growth can happen exponentially over time. You will actually attract the right energy and see things changing before your very eyes when you make a decision and commit to change. The next place in our journey may seem overwhelming, but just take one step and work towards that one. Then take the next small step after that. Most importantly, just do something and keep the momentum going, building those resilience muscles! Our future selves will thank us!

Sonya Drayer has a spirit of encouragement, strong desire to help others and is passionate about continuous improvement and personal growth. She has over 23 years of experience leading and managing people through the various cross functional experience she has had in Human Resources, Real Estate, Facilities Management, Operations and Supply Chain. Drayer holds a bachelor's degree in Mechanical Engineering and a master's degree in Supply Chain and Global Operations. Drayer also serves on the Board of Directors at her church.

Sonya is currently a Supplier Performance Manager in the Aerospace & Defense industry. She utilizes her skillsets and background to develop Suppliers and institute continuous improvement strategies to develop world class business processes and partnerships with our industry partners.

Sonya is a speaker and coach to many women in various life stages. She is determined to see that women see the power and strength in the stories, their experiences and the resilience each of them has inside them.

Contact:
drayersonya7@gmail.com

9

Resilience to Keep Moving Forward

Ucheonye Maple

If there is no enemy within, the enemy outside can do you no harm.

MY DEFINITION OF brilliance is being able to stand out in a crowded space. I always say, "Shine Bright," meaning we should not be afraid to showcase the gifts and abilities we are given or operate in our natural geniuses. I love the saying: "Why fit in when you are meant to stand out?" Being able to showcase our brilliance illuminates our God-given gifts with ease. Unfortunately, for many of us, in our early childhood, we get programmed to dim our light; we hear it from our parents, from our teachers, and even from our friends. When we naturally display our behaviors, such as being a leader, we are told we are bossy, or if we ask questions, we are told we are too nosy or if we talk often, we are told we talk too much. However, everyone notices when we begin to find ourselves and love ourselves, and the brilliant minds that we have developed are brought to the surface and to the front. We must make sure we don't retreat back to the shadows but step forward towards the light.

There were times I hesitated to allow the brilliance within me to shine. I finally stood up to those individuals who tried to dim that brilliance by taking control of how I showed up at every opportunity. Once I spoke and stood up for myself, those who sought to intimidate me were silenced, and it never happened again. Speaking and standing up during those times released the power of resilience inside me.

To determine the role resilience plays in discovering our best strengths, we must first define resilience. Resilience means being able to withstand or recover quickly from difficult conditions. When we are resilient, any stress we may have is replaced with courage and perseverance.

Being resilient made me aware that I do not hold grudges. When something problematic is happening in my life, I am already planning how to get out of the situation to make it less complicated. My father passed away in 1985, leaving my mom to rear seven children as a single parent and educator. Life for us wasn't easy. I believe, because of growing up in an environment where I had six siblings, and my mother was trying to make ends meet, I had to be able to bounce back quickly from those difficult conditions. If I did not bounce back, I could have easily allowed my environment to overtake me.

I adapted the behavior of being able to think two steps ahead because of my childhood. So, whenever I'm faced with any challenge, my mind never focuses on what is happening right now; it is always focused on what could be in the future. With this mindset, I have always been able to create the wins I want in my life-unapologetically.

Learning to Shine

Multiple people in my life encouraged me to shine. First, my mom used to tell me all the time, "Uche, I was never worried about you." During my high school years, she would say, "When you got off from work, you always did your home-work." Mom continued to say, "I never had to worry about your grades." Her faith in me was great, but I had to learn about being resilient even in high school. There are so many distractions in high school, and it was imperative to have a goal and remain focused on it regardless of the challenges that may incur.

When I met my husband in my early 20s, I didn't know that I could accomplish the things that I did. My husband used to tell me, "You have no idea how much power you have." I never knew what that meant, but over the years, he continued to say it and I began to believe it. He continues to remind me that there is something almost magical about me. My husband lovingly reiterates, "Your power in how you come into a room, in how you engage with people, com-mands presence. Even when you communicate, it makes people listen."

My husband's comments made me think about how I could harness the power of my talents. I was volunteering for a non-profit, and I had the role of being Program's Chair. It was my responsibility to hold professional development events and community services events through the city in this role. One community service event that I gave birth to was Thanksgiving at the Ronald McDonald House. This was the first time we had ever done an event like this. The goal was to provide a Thanksgiving environment for families living at the Ronald McDonald House by cooking and engaging with the families whose loved ones were in the hospital. After weeks of planning, organizing, and managing, the day finally arrived, and it was a huge success. We had so much food, an abundance of volunteers, and so many families were in attendance; it was a hit. After the event, I received many compliments on how I managed and planned such a successful event with such a great turnout. I knew I had tapped into my area of genius, but I still did not understand how to harness that power yet.

In my 30's I was starting a new job as a manager, and within my first week, I knew I needed a mentor that would help me understand my workplace environment, the company's goals, and my department culture. A senior-level director recommended someone for me; he believed this individual would be the right one for me. I remember meeting my mentor for the first time. We met over the phone, and he was listening to what I had to say. Our first encounter would reveal if this mentorship was going to flourish or die. I say this because within the first five minutes of our conversation, I retched all of the issues and challenges I faced in my current role. He listened so quietly I had to ask twice, "are you still there?" He finally said to me, "You've got this!" He didn't know me personally at the time. Yet, he affirmed to me, "You've got this!" Over multiple years, our professional relationship grew. This mentor always reminds me that I am brilliant, and he tells me that anything I do or touch is impressive. I think this mentor solidified what my mother and husband told me. His affirmations were instrumental in my new job. Through this situation, I learned to persevere and remain resilient in that ever-changing dynamic environment.

During each decade of my life, giving myself permission to shine continues to evolve. I am now in my 40's (at the time of this book publication), and I realize how much power I can wheel. I just need to be me, and the rest will follow.

Strategies for Greatness through Family Ties

My mother never had a chance to remain knocked down. Referring to the saying, "When life beats you up, if you can look up, then you can get up." My mom always chose to get up; she kept coming back. I definitely know that watching my mom push through as a single mother with seven kids gave me the foundation to be resilient. She made sure we had an education and that we received everything we needed. My mother's resilience flowed to all my siblings as well. The key strategies my mom passed to us encompassed keeping God first, always. Secondly, she taught us to believe in ourselves even when no one else does. We learned to become our biggest advocates. Mom's belief system included believing even when what we desired in life didn't exist or had not manifested. Lastly, mom taught us that family is always essential. Together, we can work through any situation.

We tend to look at our moms as superheroes. You know, "No weapon formed against us shall prosper,[1]" and they behaved as such. Looking back at my mom's life, I am in awe of everything she has ever accomplished. A woman from East Texas, who graduated college in 3.5 years, has her first child at 20, married my dad, a Nigerian, and then decided

---

she wanted us to get international experience by moving her family to Lagos, Nigeria, for 5 years.

One major lesson I have learned from my mom is to always bet on yourself. There have been many times when I know I counted myself out, but I took the risk, and sometimes the results were fruitful, and other times they were learning lessons. The lesson I learn is to LEAP. LEAP stands for Learn to Excel and Affirm Your Power. This motto has positioned me to excel in my career quickly, retire at 44 years old, and become a successful entrepreneur.

I also witnessed my older sister's resilience while facing various trials and tribulations. She passed away of breast cancer after being cancer-free for two years. My sister was the type of person who did not like handouts. She was a diligent worker, and she taught me how to stand up to the naysayers with integrity. She also taught me how to be con-frontational with others while demonstrating truthfulness. There was never any name-calling, but the sophistication of making someone feel grossly responsible for what they did to another was her superpower. Her crucial strategic positioning was always making sure everyone had a fair chance. She did not like bullies, and she loved life. She was an advocate, willing to stand up to anyone who challenged fairness for everyone. Whenever someone was in need, she was never afraid to give a helping hand.

A person attending my sister's funeral shared this story with our family through a letter. My sister was the manager of a Taco Bell, and he came into the store with torn clothes, holes in his shoes looking for a job. The man was homeless, but he said something told him to walk into the store and apply for a job. When he asked for an application, some of the workers laughed at him, but my sister nipped that in the bud immediately. He applied for the job, and she hired him. She looked at him and said, "You can start here today. Your life starts today." He then said, "Your sister changed my life forever as a result of giving me a chance." My sister's authenticity, determination to help others, and ability to see the best in others made her resilient and a force to be reckoned with.

Brilliance and Resilience in Crisis

So many passed away in 2020 during the pandemic. I felt a sense of loss and then, like the rest of the world, we experienced the death of George Floyd on national television. It was so much happening around me that I didn't realize I was having a personal crisis. Sometimes we pray prevailing prayers, but we need to pray "just get me through this" prayers. While seeking to be resilient, I knew I needed to just push through the moment. More than bouncing back quickly, I felt I needed to work through the emotions caused by these crises to gain stability.

I sought the aid of a therapist because I had anxiety attacks. I couldn't go outside because I was visualizing what could possibly happen to my boys based on the tragedy of George Floyd. The therapist did one exercise that thoroughly helped me. Even though I got through the crisis, I still use this exercise occasionally. My therapist asked if I believe in God or some other higher power, and I said yes. She then said, "What color would that be? If God is around you, what color would that be?" I said, "That would be blue." She then responded, "OK, all the stuff that's inside of you that needs to come out, what color would that be?" I said, "Red." She then replied, "Visualize this: When you're breathing God, it is blue, and when you exhale, you are releasing all the negativity as red." As a result of that exercise, walking, praying, and looking at life half full instead of half empty, I gradually got out of the negativity I created. I was no longer snared by self-isolation. I just imagined that I was continuously inhaling God's presence and exhaling the fear, isolation, and anxiety. There is nothing more biblical than knowing your entire being is covered by God's omniscience.

During that time, I was strengthened and became a better leader because of self-awareness and self-reflection. As leaders, we must be aware of what is happening at the moment and assess it. While walking through that moment, we must stop to reflect on where we are now and where we need to be so that we can eternalize in ourselves the progress we have made that may not be seen but is felt.

I am more in tune with others' behavior, including those who work with me because of my experience. I now have a greater sense of discernment, which allows me to make better decisions because of what I went through in 2020.

Navigation, Trial & Error, and Purpose

One of my mottos is to "be a light in the midst of darkness." I believe my purpose is to always give back. I discovered my purpose by navigating the ridges using trial and error because I was rejected. Part of the opportunity to give back is to help STEM (science, technology, engineering, and mathematics) professionals, especially women, advance in the marketplace. My goal is to encourage these women to remain in the STEM industry because we need their brilliance in the workplace.

In 2015, I was working an abundance of hours on my job. I was highly stressed, and I was overworked. A new position opened at my workplace. I applied, but I did not get it. I was disappointed and angry because I felt I was qualified. Another position became available, and I applied for it as well. Again, I was overlooked for the job. I became "sick and tired" of hearing, "you are not what I am looking for," "maybe next time," or "you need more experience." The moment I got the last rejection notice, I decided, "that was enough!" I took ownership of my career because I knew my worth. That Sunday, I saw an opportunity external to the company; I applied and was scheduled for an interview the next day. On Friday of that week, I received an offer, and my packet was ready a week later.

I was then placed in a position where I could hire others. Hearing the stories of diverse women who were rejected, I knew in my heart, "this must stop." I knew it was my responsibility to make sure qualified women were not denied an opportunity under my watch. I became more intentional in my mission and purpose. My mission now is to coach and mentor 100,000 women in the STEM industry. If I had not received those rejections, I now realize that I would not be who I am today. I would not have started my leadership and personal development training company.

Challenges and Triumphs

One of my most significant challenges was graduating high school. It was not related to academics but my personal home life. My stepfather was sick with an addiction. Watching his addiction affect our family from the time I was a junior in high school through my senior year was challenging. It tore my family apart relative to the unnecessary chaos. We dealt with theft around our house and constant disorder.

I believe I was able to persevere and remain resilient because I took all that negative energy and chaos from my home life and focused it on excelling in high school so I could leave home. I knew if I graduated high school successfully, that would be my ticket out. When I graduated high school and college, I left Texas with the intention of never returning. My plans were to leave all those situations behind and start somewhere else fresh and new.

Before my mother remarried, I grew up in a Christian home, attending church services five days a week. The situation with my stepfather disrupted the foundational core of who we were as a family. So, as a young woman, I took all that disruptive energy and focused it on school and told myself, "If not now, when? You can get out of this and create your own destiny." I can remember the moment I decided I would no longer be a voluntary victim but become a victor in my current situation. It is true you have to make lemonade out of lemons, but it is also true that you may need to add more sugar to remove the sour taste.

Helping Others on the Road to Success

I started mentoring my family for as long as I can remember. I have a very close relationship with my younger brother. He recently started his own construction business, and it is fruitful. I talk to him regularly about positioning himself to create wealth for his daughter, grandchildren, great-grandchildren generationally. Seeing him flourish is such a rewarding experience, and his tenacity is a force to be reckoned with. I guided him on the secrets of being wealthy and how our money should work for us and not us work for our money. It is such a pleasure to see his moves that will position his bloodline for many years to come.

I meet with one of my mentees bi-weekly. These sessions started because I noticed the mentee's behavior during a crucial conversation with a leader in a corporate meeting. After the meeting, I went to her and noted her actions. I then asked if she would participate in a workshop called "Crucial Conversations for Leaders" with me one-on-one. She agreed, and during one of our sessions, she told me I was a natural pusher or a catalyst to help get others started.

This mentee is now writing a book, and she started her own company. She said these achievements happened because we had that initial conversation. In this mentee's instance, these outcomes occurred because she had a crucial conversation where she did not back down.

When people are faced with challenges in an uncomfortable space, I use it as an opportunity to help them become more resilient. I take the uncomfortable situation and use it as a positive to push them beyond their comfort zone.

Foundational Keys to Resilience and Brilliance

The first key to discovering the brilliance within is self-awareness. We must ask ourselves, "What is someone constantly telling us we are good at doing?" We must listen and act on it.

The second key is removing the fear of failure. We should not be afraid to fail. Resilience is built, and brilliance is revealed during times of failure.

Thirdly, do not be afraid to release your authentic self. We must not allow others to rob us of our authenticity just because we are different.

"A journey of a thousand miles begins with a single step – Lao Tzu." That first step is crucial to discovering who we are and our capabilities. Take that step because when we are shifting to purpose, we are executing or getting something done. Then, we must be consistent with the plan we developed and enjoy the ride along the way with the people we meet on the journey.

Ucheonye Maple is the Managing Director of Aghaeze-Maple Enterprises, LLC, a leadership and personal development training company. Maple has more than 22 years of experience in manufacturing, systems engineering, program management and diversity and inclusion. She has worked at Fortunate 100 hundred companies that allowed her to support product development from concept to operations.

Maple is a leader with a proven track record of empowering, motivating, and transforming the lives of STEM professionals. She is a professional speaker, coach, and mentor in the STEM community. Maple is also the Founder of The Exceptional Leader University, an executive style training and coaching company for women in engineering. Her mission is to coach and mentor 100,000 women in the STEM field to reduce the number of women leaving STEM and increase the number of women in C-Suite positions.

Uche received her B.S. in Mechanical Engineering from Prairie View A&M University, MBA from University of Phoenix, and her M.S. in Systems Engineering from Johns Hopkins University. She is also a graduate from the Leadership Essentials Program at Loyola University.

Contact Information:
Ucheonye Maple, Owner of Aghaeze-Maple Enterprises, Engineering Program Manager: www.ucheonyemaple.com
umaple@ucheonyemaple.com

10

My Keyring of Resilience

Marlon Harmon

FROM THE TIME I arrived on this earth until the present, I now realize I was destined to live a life of resilience. My first experience with resiliency occurred at birth because I was born to a mom with only a fifth-grade education. My mother left the state of Mississippi and traveled to Kenosha, Wisconsin, when she was sixteen years old, seeking a better life for herself. At twenty-seven years old, she gave birth to me, her third son and fourth child, Marlon Harmon. Mom's lack of education was challenging for me because I did not understand the value of a traditional education growing up. At age four old, I was abducted by a person in our community. Screaming for my life, a nearby cousin heard me and came running to my rescue. That experience left an indelible imprint upon my life that could have taken me down a road with a different outcome, preventing me from becoming the person I am today. However, that four-year-old little boy stepped into an adult reality of the world of resilience and learned early how to overcome difficult circumstances. Reflecting back, that frightening experience opened the door to the first key to resilience I would need later in life. The Endurance Key was added to my keyring. I went into survival mode, and I am a survivor. However, there was also an element of trauma that was not unlocked or removed from my consciousness that remained with me throughout my life.

By the grace of God, I was not entrapped in bitterness for what happened to me. I still carried a heart of passion for others. I realized that at the age of nineteen when that same individual who abducted me was released from jail into a halfway house where I worked. I remember that day when I unexpectedly walked into work and saw he was a new tenant in the house. Walking into the hallway, I recalled that individual coming out of a community room and facing me eye to eye for the first time since my horrifying experience. My reaction expressed shock and concern while demonstrating a sense of resolve. I immediately went to the supervisor of the halfway house and shared that I could not work there with that individual. The supervisor gave me time off from that shift while they resolved the problem. Within 24 hours, my abductor was moved to another facility.

As an adult, I could have responded differently and retaliated against that person because of what he did to me. But God's sustaining grace helped me keep my composure because He gave me a different temperament. I am reminded of the scripture in Jeremiah 1:5 NIV (New International Version) that says, "Before I formed you in the womb I knew you, before you were born I set you apart..."[1] The person God placed in

---

[1] Jeremiah 1:5. THE HOLY BIBLE, NEW INTERNATIONAL VERSION® Copyright© 1973, 1978, 1984, 20111, by Biblica, Inc.™. Used by permission of Zondervan.

my mother's womb is the same individual He continues to have His hand upon, wiring me just the way I am. God gave me a great love for humanity, and even when I am upset with someone, those feeling do not last for long periods of time. I went home from work that day, and when I returned the next day, I was ready to move forward. That experience added the Grace Key to my Keyring of Resilience. I understood there was pain and hurt in that experience, but those emotions did not end with destruction. I grew from that moment, knowing I could face a tough challenge and still forge ahead with my life.

The Education Key

An additional key on my Keyring of Resilience was developed while living with my grandmother. My mom was incarcerated, and my siblings and I had to move in with her mom. I faced learning challenges in school because I started reading at a later age than my peers. I had difficulty understanding the content and the placement of the content while reading. I was an underdeveloped reader, and the cause of my problems was not immediately diagnosed. (It was not determined until my eleventh-grade year of high school that I had a form of dyslexia.) The school system placed me in the Chapter One (later called Title One) reading program during the first grade. Even though I had extra help, reading was still a challenge for me, so I did not want to go to school. I did not want to face the stigma of being separated from my peers while learning. I made excuses to my grandmother as to why I could not go to school. Many times, I faked an illness. My grandmother, who pampered me well as her baby, did not force the issue. She believed whatever I said.

Reflecting on that key, I realize education is the foundation of every individual's life. The Education Key builds character and helps define the potential future outcome of an individual's standing or placement in society. I did not understand that in kindergarten and through elementary school. Thus, I ended up repeating the third grade.

When I received that last report card in the third grade, I remember walking down the longest block of my life to get to my house. A group of kids from my neighborhood were standing outside the Bedford family home directly across the road from our house. They were all chatting, laughing, and just having fun as they planned how they would spend the summer. As I got closer to the Bedford's house, they called me over to ask me about passing to the next grade. There was such a deep heaviness as I opened my mouth to say I had to repeat the third grade.

However, it was not the neighbors or the friends in the crowd that made fun of me. It was my older brother who coined a phrase and called me flunky. His reaction had such a profound impact on my life. Though hurtful, that moment became the key that started the ignition to the turning point of my life. At the time, I did not realize how resolved I became to make sure the name flunky did not plant itself permanently in my spirit, mind, and imagination.

Today, my brother Dewayne and I can laugh about that statement. As an adult, I returned to Kenosha, and my brother and I took a photo at the very spot that event in my life happened. Those school years were a painful period in my life, and it was tough to handle as a child. I could not understand situations back then that I realize their significance now that I am older. That Education Key and repeating the third grade took me across the great racial divide (Lincoln Park) in Kenosha and introduced me to my new best friend and another key on my Keyring of Resilience.

The Key of Hope and Perseverance

While repeating the third grade, I befriended Pat Ennis. Pat's parents were active in scouting. They embraced me as part of their family, and I became part of the Scouting Program. Over time, I grew from a Cub Scout to the Webelos and ultimately became an Eagle Scout. The will to persevere to the level of Eagle Scout was a crucial key on my Keyring of Resilience. I did not use my learning disability as an excuse. Becoming a scout allowed me the privilege to take that success as an adult and use it in my current resume while utilizing all the skillsets I learned on the journey. The experiences gained from traveling around the country, attending campouts, and my first National Jamboree were monumental in my life. During my first National Jamboree, I had the privilege of seeing First Lady Nancy Reagan, the guest speaker that year. That is the closest I have ever gotten to a national leader of these great United States of America.

During that trip to the National Jamboree, I witnessed for the first time people who looked like me who had beautiful homes and what appeared to be successful careers. That experience added another key to my Keyring of Resilience and accelerated a desire within my belly to become more than a blue-collar factory worker in Kenosha. I only had one thought before that visualization of what was happening outside of my small world and community in Kenosha. I would follow the legacy of my community and go to work at America Motors Corporation, where there was a work again – off again mentality. But seeing those successful African Americans in Washington DC gave me hope.

When I think of Jeremiah 29:11, I understand from a very personal place in my life, that God has a plan for me. It was a hope for a future that would never harm me. ["For I know the plans I have for you," declares the Lord, "plans to prosper you and not to harm you, plans to give you hope and a future." Jeremiah 29:11 NIV][2] Prior to my Washington DC excursion, I never knew what it was like to hope for anything. However, I had experienced healthy envy towards people in my community who I assumed were better off than the Harmons. I did not know there were more opportunities available for me, and there were keys to being brilliant. It took those encounters with the Ennis family and the Scout Program to change the rusty keys I previously owned and find more brilliant keys to add to my keyring.

During that time, I even developed a desire to become a member of the foreign service. There was a new desire to travel and meet more people from all over the world like I experienced at the National Jamboree, where we traded merit badges with scouts from other countries. I also exchanged scarves and other memorabilia with people from Nepal and other parts of the world and the United States.

The Treasure Key

The Key of Hope and Perseverance led to another door that allowed me to go beyond the borders of Kenosha, Wisconsin. Although I did not know I was dyslexic at the time, I remember transitioning into junior high school that year after coming back from the jamboree. Thus, I received an additional key because of a new relationship with a woman named Louise Lovdahl. Louise came into my life at age 14 when she became my Junior High School Music and Study Hall teacher. She was so convinced that there was something special about Marlon Harmon, and the key she provided to me was what I call the Treasure Key.

---

[2]Jeremiah 29:11. THE HOLY BIBLE, NEW INTERNATIONAL VERSION® Copyright© 1973, 1978, 1984, 20111, by Biblica, Inc.™. Used by permission of Zondervan.

Louise recognized I had academic struggles. But once she determined I had a gift for public speaking, Louise wanted me to improve my skills. While taking part in a program called "I Took the Pledge," Louise allowed me to be a spokesman for the organization giving me a chance to travel to other schools and share about our program.

Through the "I Took the Pledge" program, I also participated in a "Just so No" parade in Chicago, Illinois, where we joined with Chicago Bears football players like Walter Payton, David Duerson, Jim McMahon, and Michael Singletary. At the time, these football players were known for their widely acclaimed Superbowl Shuffle Video. These same Chicago Bears football players privately came to Kenosha, and in a small studio filmed with the "I Took the Pledge" group, a video called "The Pledger Shuffle." That experience in Chicago gave me the confidence hidden inside the Treasure Key, letting me know I could stand publicly and speak articulately. The Treasure Key continues to play a significant role in my life, reminding me of who I am in the Lord. I know there are treasures inside all of us to be used to help change the world for the better. Today, I use that Treasure Key as I speak professionally as a minister and as a trainer and facilitator.

A Life Changing Keyring

Applying my Endurance, Education, Treasure, and Hope and Perseverance keys, I attended college. Yes, it was a challenge, and it required resilience and brilliance. But my Psychology professor, Dr. Larry Hamilton at Carthage College, saw the brilliance inside me, and he used his "out of the box" thinking to encourage me and push me forward.

After not scoring well on one of my tests, Dr. Hamilton once said to me, "Quite frankly, you are perplexing to me.

But I am not done because even though it doesn't come out on your examinations, there is no way we can have these dialogs, and you can participate in this classroom if you didn't have the knowledge and understanding of the content." "I say this because you can stand toe to toe with your peers."

Beyond completing college, my Keyring of Resilience I started acquiring from birth is being used to tell my story with the renowned group of authors of this book. This book project gives me continual hope for my future and my family's future. I try to use the keys on my Keyring of Resilience to share with everyone else that we can take our past and leverage it for our future. We can take past hurt and turn them into future prosperity. We can take past challenges and use them to produce greater success on our journey.

My Keyring of Resilience is likened to an experience I had when my older brother, Vincent visited me in Arizona. He and I decided to take a 75-mile bike ride. While on the journey, we realized it would take us longer and require more endurance than we thought to return to our starting point that happened to be my car. During the last part of the journey back, I realized the physical tank in my body was empty. Five miles from where I knew my vehicle was parked, I practically bottomed out regarding my energy level. There was no reserve in me, and the only thing I had left was the vision of my destination. That vision was the resiliency I was able to leverage to keep my eyes focused on reaching my car so that I could force my body to keep paddling.

When we reach the place where we think all is done, we have no more hope, and we are empty physically and emotionally, and there is no one to assist us; we must rely on the vision until it comes to fruition. Using my Keyring of

Resilience aided me in making it back to my car and completing our journey. Even for a person who feels they have no hope, I believe that they can leverage themselves to the next phase of life with the right keys on their Resilience Keyring.

A shift influencer and pivot master **Marlon Harmon** holds a BA in Psychology from Carthage College and an M. Ed. in Leadership from Northern Arizona University. Born and raised in Kenosha, Wisconsin, by his great grandmother (Big Mama), Marlon was poured into at an early age the gifting in the pivot along with how to push past your dreams and pull them into reality through a resilient, focused attitude and work ethic. Marlon's resolve for better ignited in the sixth grade and has not slowed yet. Marlon holds the honor of being an Eagle Scout and a Nominee of the White House Fellowship. He believes the most significant titles he holds are being a Licensed and Ordained Minister of the Gospel and being called husband and father.

Contact Information:
www.btchgroup.com or btcngroup@gmail.com

11

Walking in My Truth

Odetta Scott

AS A LEADER, it is not about me. Leaders must lead effectively, bringing people along, building them up to grow and develop. It should be a leader's goal to help those whom they serve to find their inner brilliance, particularly when they experience some form of adversity.

When I think of resiliency, I also think of mentoring. That means pouring into people. I have the opportunity to mentor many accomplished women and men. These talented ladies and gentlemen sometimes feel uncomfortable, challenged, or need encouragement. As their mentor, I use these challenging moments to nurture them forward. Resiliency is a foundational cornerstone that helps us discover our best strengths...our best self. Resiliency stretches us to be more and perform better than we ever thought we could. Additionally, resiliency serves as a motivator, which personally teaches me the importance of life-long learning.

As a life-long learner and Certified Six Sigma Black Belt,

my journey has not been easy. As part of the certification program, I had to present to a group of Vice Presidents across the company. My first presentation was not successful because I tried to present an entire project when I only had ownership of a portion of it. I was very devastated and disappointed. However, my disappointment and frustration led to a vital learning opportunity. After carefully noting my mistakes, I looked for viable solutions.

For my second attempt, I owned every aspect of the project. It was a different project, and I orchestrated multiple board meetings, using them as "prep sessions" before the final presentation. I walked in confident and prepared and felt like no one else knew the project better than me. I knew that "God had not given me the spirit of fear; but of power, and of love, and of a sound mind."[1] The Vice Presidents of the organization gave me a paramount compliment at the second presentation. They called me an energized change agent! It was music to my ears and very gratifying to know that I could achieve my goal learning from my previous mistakes, course correcting as necessary, and being persistent. I received my black belt certification during the second presentation. The experience of having a less than desirable outcome (Board 1) and pivoting to implement learning and make the outcome (Board 2) a success continues to inspire me and helps me to inspire others.

Being Inspired and Inspiring Others

There are multiple people who inspired me and helped me discover my inner brilliance. Bettye Brown was one of those

---

[1]Taken from 2 Timothy 1:7. King James Bible. (2020). King James Bible Online. https://www.kingjamesbibleonline.org.

people. She was like an aunt to me, encouraging me to be any-thing that I wanted to be. Bettye called me her "Phenomenal Woman," inspired by Maya Angelou's poem. After Bettye passed in 2020, her words are something that I hold near and dear to my heart. The essence of Angelou's poem… "rejects narrow societal expectations of women and proposes an alternative perspective on what defines real beauty. Confidence and comfort in one's own skin, [Angelou insists], are the markers of true beauty, and the poem offers an empowering message for all women."[2] Betty's belief and encouragement helped me understand that it is OK to be different and be proud of who I am and what I have to offer. Regardless of how small I think it is, my thoughts still add value.

Being my authentic self is a large portion of my char-acter. It is very challenging and takes a lot of energy to be someone else. My name is distinctive and extraordinarily unique. The only other Odetta that I am aware of is the folk singer, Odetta Holmes, an African American "classically trained folk, blues and gospel singer,"[3] who also used her voice as a civil and human rights activist. Odetta Holmes passed in 2008. Growing up, I did not like my name (one of my differences), and I threatened to change it when I turned 18. As I matured and got older, I began to appreciate the uniqueness of my name. Also, after doing some research on the name Odetta, I realized it means wealthy.[4] So, every time someone calls my name, they are calling me wealthy.

From a biblical perspective, the names mentioned in the Bible were reflective of a person's life and purpose. For example,

---

[2] LitCharts Website. (Viewed 2021). https://www.litcharts.com/poetry/maya-angelou/phenome-nal-woman.

[3] Wikipedia website. (Viewed 2021). https://en.wikipedia.org/wiki/Odetta.

[4] Think Baby Names Website. (Viewed 2021). http://www.thinkbabynames.com/meaning/0/Odette.

Abraham's wife, Sarah, was initially named Sarai, meaning "my princess." However, once it was foretold that she would no longer be barren but birth a son in her old age, God instructed Abraham to call her Sarah, meaning "Princess."[5] Sarah would no longer be considered as just Abraham's princess, but as he became the father of many nations, she would be known from a worldwide biblical perspective as "a *mother of nations*."[6]

For me, the name Odetta goes beyond the financial meaning of wealth. As a woman in the STEM industry, I gained a wealth of knowledge that allows me to help shape a population of other women in STEM. While in college, I aspired to become an astronaut, paving the way to mentor women in science. However, a medical illness prevented my dreams from coming forth. Although that dream was denied, I have been given the honor to pour into others as an engineer through my efforts and mantra of "each one reach one." My God-given passion to better myself and others is a catalyst that fuels my mentoring activities in organizations such as Leading Inspired Females in Technology (LIFT) and the Society of Women Engineers (SWE), in addition to the 20-plus years of working in the Aerospace and Defense industry. Yes, the dream of becoming an astronaut may have been denied. But, the resiliency to forge ahead as a female engineer opened greater doors to inspire others to discover their brilliance. From that viewpoint, I am a wealthy woman!

Resilient Inspirators

Looking over my life, I have been inspired by many other resilient people. Some I know personally, others I watched

---

[5] Taken from Genesis 17: 15. King James Bible. (2020). King James Bible Online. https://www.king-jamesbibleonline.org.

[6] Taken from Genesis 17: 16–17. King James Bible. (2020). King James Bible Online. https://www.kingjamesbibleonline.org.

from afar. Daniel Scott, Jr. (my partner, husband, and blessing), President Obama, Mother Teresa, Nelson Mandela, and Martin Luther King Jr are a few of those people. Regardless of the challenges and hardships these people encountered, they still got up, dusted themselves off, and drove to make a positive impact. Each of them demonstrated consistency, learning from their challenges and course-correcting to get better.

During Barack Obama's Presidency, in his 2009 campaign speech, he passionately wanted to "turn the page" to restore the economy, keep the country out of new entangling wars, and find a way to govern across the partisan divide. But he encountered formidable obstacles. If we go back to 2015, President Obama delivered a eulogy in Charleston, South Carolina, after the mass shooting in a church there. As he neared the end, he took a long pause and then began singing "Amazing Grace." It was an unforgettable, transcendent moment and brought the audience to their feet, based on their ability to connect and understand what that truly means "Amazing Grace."[7] When I look at the recording today, it brings me to chills. President Obama also made inspirational statements after the heartbreaking mass shootings in Tucson, Aurora, Newtown, Charleston, Roseburg, San Bernardino, and Orlando during his Presidency. As a leader of the United States of America, I am sure these shootings took a toll on him, as I would expect they did on us all. In the position of President and still being able to push forward, understanding that we must be "United" to me shows resiliency.

My husband Daniel overcame four F's in college at Purdue University to become a great business and community

---

[7] Ignatius, David. The Washington Post. (2016, June 16).

leader, husband and father. Through this less than desirable situation, Daniel found the resilience within to triumph and finish his degree in engineering.

Mother Teresa dedicated her life to serving the poor and destitute around the world. In 1979 she was awarded the Nobel Peace Prize. Her strengths include her focus and dedication to the core mission of her organization – helping the poorest of the poor. She was considered a great listener and focused a great deal on helping others grow.[8] I consider her amongst the greatest of servant leaders.

Nelson Mandela inspired me because of his self-sacrifice. He spent 27 years in prison, and when offered freedom, he refused, saying, "I cannot and will not give any undertaking, at a time when I and you, the people, are not free. Your freedom and mine cannot be separated!"[9] A leader that does the right thing regardless of the impact on him personally. I think that is very inspiring. Nelson Mandela was a servant-leader who sought to unify and empower his people, not just those already in power or those without, but everyone. He was also very humble. Though others stood in awe of his sacrifice, he continued to emphasize: "My first task when I came out was to destroy that myth that I was something other than an ordinary human being."[10]

Dr. Martin Luther King was a successful leader of the African American civil rights movement in the United States. He galvanized society through his use of Mahatma Gandhi's nonviolence approach and his oratory skills to move the needle on racism. Characteristics that made him a great

---

[8]Devasahayam, MG. (2016, September 5). The Straits Times. https://www.straitstimes.com/asia/south-asia/mother-teresa-a-true-servant-leader-the-statesman-columnist

[9]Dhliwayo, Matshona. (2017, August 8). 7 Reasons Why Nelson Mandela Was a Great Leader. https://medium.com/@matshonatdhliwayo/7-reasons-why-nelson-mandela-was-a-great-leader-by-matshona-dhliwayo-203fdab12b03.

[10]Dhliwayo, Matshona. (2017, August 8).

leader include (but are not limited to) his ability to dream big, persuade without power, give people something to believe in, embrace fear and be courageous anyway, get everyone involved, create a sense of urgency, and inspire people.[11]

Keys to Discovering the Brilliance Within

On my path to discovering brilliance, I uncovered multiple keys I believe can be used by anyone willing to go through the utilization process. The first of these keys is "Becoming More Self-aware." If you get knocked down (feel like you have failed), don't stay down. Brush yourself off and get up. Let the learning from the less successful engagement drive you, course-correct, and knock it out of the park.

There is an approach or skill I call reframing. I consider myself a very positive person. Along with the "each one reach one mantra," I start each day with a positive approach...Magnificent Monday, Terrific Tuesday, Wonderful Wednesday, Thankful Thursday, and Fantastic Friday!... Now, back to reframing. I define reframing as the ability to take a scenario or a situation and express it differently, taking the negative and looking at it through a different lens. For example, you may first say, "I had a goal of completing six training classes. However, I did not complete all six training courses." With reframing, the statement could be, "I completed three of the six courses, and I plan on completing the remaining three courses in three weeks."

I shared a personal life-changing experience of reframing in the book Women in Leadership – Living Beyond Challenges.[12]

[11]Kerpen, Dave. (Viewed 2021, October). 7 Simple Entrepreneurship Lessons from Martin Luther King. Inc. https://www.inc.com/dave-kerpen/7-simple-entrepreneurship-lessons-from-martin-luther-king.html.

12 Goodson, Amanda and Rice, Yvette. (2019). *Women in Leadership – Living Beyond Challenges.* United States. Amanda Goodson Global, LLC. 153 – 156.

It all started back in my preadolescent years when I decided I wanted to be an astronaut. Something about the uniqueness of the career, the hard work it would take to attain it, and the reward it would bring excited me. I constructed a plan to meet my lofty goal, taking advanced math and science courses throughout my school years that not only satisfied academic requirements but served to set me apart from my classmates. I needed to excel. I knew my attitude, behavior, and work ethic would help set the stage for what I wanted to achieve.

In 1987, when I first heard Mae Jemison (the first female African American to go into space) had become one of the 15 candidates NASA selected out of more than 2,000 people to enter training to become an astronaut, I was elated. To know that a role model who shared my ethnicity, gender, and aspiration was on the path to accomplishing what I wanted so badly was encouraging. As I followed Mae's progress, I left my home in Vicksburg, Mississippi, in eleventh grade to attend a magnet school in Columbus, Mississippi, to enhance my education. That decision forced me to grow up fast without my parents or family, become more self-aware, and make new friends, contacts, and networks. From there, I attended the U.S. Naval Academy in Annapolis, Maryland (as most astronauts at that time were trained in the U.S. Navy) through my sophomore year before moving on to Texas A&M University to finish college and earn my degree in mechanical engineering technology in 1995.

My time at the Academy was bittersweet. The program provided much-needed structure and discipline, and I successfully completed my plebe (freshman) year, which most consider to be the hardest. I am very proud of this accomplishment. However, towards the completion of the following year, I began to experience severe medical issues. I was in and out of the hospital, and doctors could not determine the root cause. I did some soul searching and decided that I was sacrificing my health to get a better education. My family was far away and not able to come and be with me as I was ailing physically with no precise diagnosis of what was wrong. During this time, I leaned into God and grew in my faith. It taught me that when things don't turn out as we thought they would, there is still a greater plan in motion: God's plan!

By the third hospital stay, I realized I wasn't going into space like Mae did aboard the Space Shuttle Endeavor in 1992—but I figured I'd do the next best thing as an engineer by helping send others up and giving myself more visibility within the field in the process. I didn't complete my time at the Naval Academy, but resiliency and determination were added and reemphasized as building blocks for my life. It all served as a catalyst for my positive attitude and approach and made "each one reach one" a reality in and through my life. After leaving the Academy, I still had a few more medical episodes, but they eventually ended without ever being diagnosed.[13]

The second key comes after reframing. It involves turning the reframed experience into an advantage. Becoming an engineer was advantageous for me relative to mentoring

---

[13]Goodson, Amanda and Rice, Yvette. (2019). *Women in Leadership – Living Beyond Challenges.* United States. Amanda Goodson Global, LLC. 153 – 156.

more women in the STEM industry. The passion for focusing on Diversity, Equity, and Inclusion (DE&I) for women grew with every opened door and promotion I experienced in the STEM industry and has continued for more than 25 years. I have chaired the Leading Inspired Females in Technology (LIFT) Advocacy Council, Recognition & Retention Committee for a major Fortune 100 STEM corporation, helping to deploy Knowledge Cafés (focus groups) across the organization nationally and internationally. The mission of LIFT is to enable women in STEM to obtain extraordinary outcomes by bringing their authentic selves to work daily.

In addition to LIFT program, I am serving as the Development Programs Chair of the Engineering African American Advocacy Council (EAAAC) for the same Fortune 100 STEM corporation. The EAAAC focuses on building a sustainable and diverse workforce, strengthening the pipeline of African American Engineering talent for the corporation by creating and providing tools for its members. Yet another means for moving a reframed situation into an advantageous moment in the lives of other people, the original goal I desired to achieve as an astronaut.

Resilience and Continuous Growth Through Crises and Beyond

During a crisis, I intentionally drive consistency with learning, even from my challenges. I course correct accordingly, especially from those testing encounters. From a young age, my mother and father made sure I had a knowledgeable faith in God. Thus, my spiritual journey provides an avenue of strength and resiliency regardless of the crises. Today, my faith in God is one of the core values that reminds me of who I am and how I live, along with integrity, authenticity, and character. I see character as the ability to stand strong in the midst of the storm and still do the right thing, even when the right thing may not be popular.

I also make sure I am taking time for myself and reassessing my plans for progress regularly. I ask myself, "How will you strengthen your skills and become a greater leader?" during those most challenging times. Additionally, I look for courses that I can take for continuous improvement, learning more about social media aspects and how to leverage those skills learned for a win/win situation.

Even during a crisis, I continue to reach out and help others. My mantra, "each one reach one," is still operative during these times because I know I did not get to where I am alone. How can I not help someone else?

Crises usually bring changes in any scenario. During the COVID-19 pandemic, organizations and companies worldwide were affected, which meant changes in those companies were inevitable. According to the article "Driving Change through Learning," "Taking inspiration from the healthcare organization, keeping the energy high during change and helping people realize they are learning through the change process is a massive opportunity that many don't intentionally capitalize upon. In short, it helps to avoid a performance dip. From those leaving as a result of the change, to those steering the organization to a new future, all can be fueled by the prospect that change brings learning and growth opportunities."[14] Thus, learning and development can motivate throughout a change process, and during crises, even with the teams I lead.

---

[14]Sparrow, Jane. (2016, October 12). Driving Change through Learning. Training Journal. https://www.trainingjournal.com

Alongside learning opportunities, encouragement and upliftment is an essential responsibility of any leader while their organization faces crises.

As we have all endured the effects of the COVID pandemic, leaders and organizations have had to be flexible and more empathetic to really understand and meet employees where they are. As a leader in a Fortune 100 Aero & Defense company, asking how an employee is and really stopping to actively listen is essential. Being there to listen right now is quite impactful for our entire organization. We have also focused more on employee well-being. I feel as though our employees are our greatest asset and competitive differentiator. We must find a way to help us all bounce back. There has to be some silver lining in this pandemic; something better must occur as a result.

Growth and development are also the means I used to discover my purpose as I navigated the ridges to achievement. Through one of those discoveries, I improved on building my self-awareness strength while better understanding my triggers, motivators, and drivers. I consider myself to be self-motivated, so keeping continuous improvement front of mind is essential to navigating the ridges of life. Also, when I feel like I am not as successful as I would like, I ask myself, "What is the lesson to be learned, and what do I need to change in order to overcome and get better?"

Sometimes those ridges to be navigated are not self-inflicted. One of the most notable situations I experienced was when I served with a manager who had a totally different leadership style than mine. This leader's style was more autocratic, meaning he was very absolute and dogmatic. His leadership style did not resonate with my team or me at that time. I had about 10 people under my leadership who reported directly to me and indirectly reported to the program manager. Being able to summon the guts to have a critical conversation with him about how his style was demoralizing took leadership courage

It took a while to break down the barrier for us to be able to work collaboratively. However, over time, it became more of a reverse mentoring relationship where I provided insights to my manager. In this case, the growth and development opportunities were two-sided. He even invited me to participate on some occasions because he thought my leadership style would be more effective than his for a specific team or project. That experience helped me grow in subsequent roles, teaching me how to work with other leaders and to be able to provide feedback in such a way that it is received rather than being opposed or rejected and neither party obtaining the desired goals.

Final Thoughts

When shifting from plan to purpose, there are a few key takeaways I found most helpful in my journey from resilience to brilliance. First and far most, stay in faith...I have very strong faith and feel that my relationship with God is a key to my success.

Secondly, be positive...everything won't always work out your way, but there is a learning experience in every situation. How you apply what you learned to pivot is essential to your growth and your success.

Thirdly, when communicating with others, listen carefully, be present as though they are the only other person in the world; and be patient, allowing them to convey their thoughts without interruption.

Finally, execute the plan that leads to purpose. Faith without action leads to the death of any opportunity for success.

Odetta Scott, MBA, MSOD, begins every day with a passion for living through her God's given purpose for betterment of self and others. An author, coach and leader, she has fueled the development of individuals at all levels as well as driven transformational culture to exceed professional and business expectations.

Odetta has worked in Operations, Engineering, Program Management and Six Sigma for major aerospace and defense businesses. She has served as a board member of the Young Men's Christian Association (YMCA) and Advancing Minorities Interest in Engineering. Odetta is also a Science, Technology, Engineering, and Mathematics (STEM) ambassador and a member of the Society of Women Engineers (SWE). She received the 2021 Diversity Leadership Award in STEM from the Women of Color in Technology organization.

Contact Information:
LinkedIn: http://linkedin.com/in/odetta-scott-58298513

Made in the USA
Middletown, DE
11 May 2022